MW01294547

Handling Crisis Situations

A GUIDE FOR THOSE IN MINISTRY

LONNIE V. SCOTT

authorHOUSE®

AuthorHouse™
1663 Liberty Drive
Bloomington, IN 47403
www.authorhouse.com
Phone: 1-800-839-8640

First published by AuthorHouse 1/14/2010

ISBN: 978-1-4490-6172-2 (e)
ISBN: 978-1-4490-6170-8 (sc)
ISBN: 978-1-4490-6171-5 (hc)

Library of Congress Control Number: 2009913948

Printed in the United States of America
Bloomington, Indiana

This book is printed on acid-free paper.

This book is dedicated to Col. E.H. "Jim" Ammerman (Retired US Army Chaplain) and his wonderful wife, Charlene.

Through your decades of dedicated service, as a chaplain and endorser, thousands of chaplains around the world are better trained and equipped for service to God and their country.

CHAPTER TITLES/ISSUES

Health/Mental Health

Family Issues

Death

Other Issues

Health/Mental Health

Chapter 1
Abortion

I was in my office going over my notes for Sunday's message when Stacey entered. "I need to talk," she said as she closed my door.

My policy has always been to have someone outside my door when I do counseling, especially with a woman, but she had entered by surprise. Just as I stood up to find someone, I noticed another person, one I knew and trusted, enter the outer office. I resumed sitting.

"You look distressed," I observed, "quite unlike you." I had known Stacey for a little less than a year, and she had been active in the chapel program.

"I am distressed, like never before in my life." She reached over and took a large wad of tissues from the box on the coffee table. "I don't know how to start."

I remained silent as she developed the courage to continue.

"I feel horrible," she said after composing herself. "About two months before I came here, I went and had an abortion."

3

Surprise must have registered on my face. I can usually keep it in check, but apparently not in this case, for she reacted to it.

"Yeah, me—I can't believe I did it, either." She dabbed her eyes some more as she continued. "I couldn't bear the thought of what my parents would say if they found out I had gotten pregnant.

I knew Stacey's mother from meeting her in the prison camp's visiting room, and she was very religious, quite conservative—and she was outspoken against abortion.

"I take it that you aren't going to tell them about this." I already knew the answer to that.

"No—not in a hundred years!" she exclaimed.

"Well, Stacey, what brings you here?" I thought I knew already. "What can I do for you?"

Stacy broke down crying again, "I feel so guilty for getting the abortion. I know I killed a baby."

UNDERSTANDING THE CRISIS

Abortion is highly controversial topic, both in political and religious circles. The primary reason is that both views are vastly diverse.

The pro-abortion or pro-choice view is that the woman who is pregnant has the right to choose what happens to her body. The zygote or fetus does not have the status of being a human being at this point, and is considered mere tissue. The pregnant woman thus has the right to have unwanted tissue legally removed from her body the way she could have unwanted fat tissue removed in a liposuction procedure.

The anti-abortion view is from the point of conception, even as cells are being formed, the womb contains a human being. The termination of the pregnancy by any intentional means is sinful, and could be considered a homicidal act. This is especially so in partial-birth abortions where the fetus is capable of living, had a medical provider not pierced the brain causing death.

In my research of the abortion topic, I discovered there are far more deaths and injuries to abortion recipients than the majority of the public is aware of. Most are due to infections received when their uterus is accidentally pierced or occasionally their colon is pierced during the same procedure.

Many girls and women believe their abortions will be conducted in state of the art medical clinics with very professional medical providers caring for them in sterile conditions. Not necessarily so, the abortion may be performed by doctors who have lost their license to practice at hospitals, and the rest of the medical staff may be inexperienced. In order to keep costs down so teenage girls can afford abortions clinics usually can't afford to hire the best.

One issue the anti-abortionist wrestle with is what to do if pregnancy risks the life of the pregnant woman. The morality of this issue is best left to the families involved. Due to variables such as level of risk, risk to both mother and fetus, family makeup (present children), and health issues, this chapter is not a proper forum for discussion of this topic.

Many organizations have services set up to provide medical, housing, food, and adoption services for pregnant women who otherwise would choose abortion. These organizations are very expensive to operate and rely on the support of donations. There are also physicians who provide services to low income women who otherwise would elect to have an abortion due to the cost of medically carrying to term.

There is one final consideration involving this topic and that is the issue of women from Christian or conservative families who become pregnant. Many of these women do not believe in abortion themselves, but they are frightened of their families' reactions to their pregnancies. Often fear of the reaction causes them to further complicate their lives by choosing to abort the baby. They then end up living with the guilt for the rest of their lives. I have counseled many women who have been caught in this dilemma. Unfortunately, most have come for guidance after the abortion.

APPLICABLE SCRIPTURE

For you created my inmost being; you knit me together in my mother's womb. I praise you because I am wonderfully made; your works are wonderful, I know that full well. My frame was not hidden from you when I was made in the secret place. When I was woven together in the depths of the earth, your eyes saw my unformed body. All the days ordained for me were written in your book before one of them came to be.

—Psalm 139:13–16

This is what the LORD says—he who made you, who formed you in the womb, and who will help you. This is what the LORD says—your Redeemer, who formed you in the womb.

—Isaiah 44:2a; 24a

Before I formed you in the womb I knew you, before you were born I set you apart.

—Jeremiah 1:5a

WHAT TO PRAY FOR

- Pray for the woman considering abortion.

- Pray for medical personnel performing abortions to repent and cease the practice.

- Pray for the woman who had an abortion to seek forgiveness.

- Pray for those providing services to women who choose to carry to term.

- Pray for the father to accept responsibility for his actions.

- Pray for the family to be supportive so the woman will not seek an abortion.

HOW TO HELP

In order to help a woman choose not to have an abortion, one must be supportive of her. Some churches and individual Christians are quick to condemn, yet many of those considering abortion or who previously had an abortion already condemned themselves. When I look in the Scriptures, Jesus didn't condemn people caught in sin, such as the woman caught in the act of adultery (John 8:2–11), or in his encounter with Zacchaeus (Luke 19:1–10). Thus we must practice love the way Jesus taught us, and Paul wrote about in 1 Corinthians 13. Not practicing this love often drives the pregnant woman to the abortion clinic or into a relationship with a young man who isn't mature enough to love or provide for her or the baby.

If a woman is pregnant and considering an abortion, one of the best things to do is have them talk with a woman who has suffered through one and its aftermath. When I was a prison chaplain at a women's prison, one of my best volunteers was a woman who had an abortion while in her late teens. When any of the inmates at the prison was considering having an abortion, the volunteer offered to speak with her, and was often successful in talking her out of it. (The prison did not have conjugal visits. The inmates arrived pregnant or became pregnant while on furlough searching for a job for after their release.) Large churches and anti-abortion resource agencies in big cities are generally able to provide a speaker for this purpose.

If you are in an area where an abortion alternative agency doesn't exist, or you are not aware of one, Bethany Christian Services will help the pregnant girl or woman receive medical care, baby clothing, furniture, formula, and other necessities. They will send counselors, regardless of how far the woman is from a crisis center. They will also help with adoption if the woman chooses this option, and they do not charge for their services. I *highly* recommend contacting Bethany Christian Services (1-800-238-4269 or www.bethany.org).

If, after all of your efforts, the woman still chooses to have the abortion, advise her not to sign any documents absolving the clinic of legal responsibility for medical malpractice. If the clinic injures her, her injuries could end up costing tens of thousands of dollars, and the clinic should be help responsible for their actions.

Local churches, even those in rural areas, have a place in this process. A young woman who becomes pregnant is going to need emotional support after making her decision—whichever decision she makes. Counseling for the woman to bring her into, or back into the family of God is the best place to start. Most of the women I have counseled, who have become pregnant out of wedlock, carry a load of guilt—especially as their pregnancy becomes more visible.

The church is also an excellent location for the pregnant girl's family and the father's family to come together and discuss the pregnancy and the financial support the father or his family should give. These meetings/counseling sessions are not a time of blaming, accusing, or finger pointing. Support of the mother and baby should be the key focus.

When it is a young couple, the father of the baby often abandons the girl and her family, and they will miss his support. Pastors or church counselors can provide education, training, and emotional support in raising a child as a single parent. They may also direct the girl to legal services that will assist in securing financial support from the father.

The church should also be where the parents and siblings go for support and healing from the shame they feel for having raised a girl "who got herself into this predicament." It is very difficult for parents who feel like failures to be supportive, and to start out as good grandparents. Small towns make the situation harder as everyone knows the family, and the family knows they are being discussed.

Pastors should also be aware of efforts by some family members to force the girl and the baby's father to get married regardless of their level of maturity or lack of love for each other. I have experienced this both as pastor and as a Navy chaplain. Taking a stand and refusing to perform a wedding for a couple that is not ready does not make a pastor popular with the family or families, however, it is the right thing to do. Eventually, the families will realize the pastor did the right thing by not performing the wedding.

If a woman has already had an abortion she will need support as well. Again, it is important to not condemn her. The church, the local church, and Christians should be viewed as her sanctuary.

If the abortion was very recent, the woman needs to be monitored for heavy or long term bleeding, serious cramping, or fever and infection. Having an abortion is not a safe procedure, the infection and injury, and the death rate is high—especially for teens. When the women exit the clinics, they are often heavily sedated and incapable of comprehending the instructions given to them by the clinicians.

Many women need counseling following an abortion. Many abortion alternative centers provide counselors. Some large churches and

Christian counseling centers have counselors experienced in post-abortion counseling. If you or a woman is in an area where counseling is not available, or you don't know where to go for a referral, I recommend contacting Project Rachel (www.hopeafterabortion.com or 1-800-593-2273). Project Rachel provides counseling over the phone. They also make referrals to centers in many areas, including rural areas. If the woman you are working with is unwilling to contact Project Rachel, I recommend you contact them. They will assist you in helping your friend or family member.

One last consideration, helping someone who is considering an abortion, or who had an abortion, is complicated work. There are many factors involved in trying to help a woman decide against having the procedure, as well as helping someone who has had one. This is one situation where you should seek professional help at the onset if you have never encountered this type of situation before. The people working at Bethany Christian Services, and agencies like Bethany, have resources to help a woman make an informed choice against abortion. They are also there to help those of us who do not have the experience and resources. They want to help, and they are excellent at what they do.

FOLLOW-UP

I set Stacey up with a post-abortion counselor who was a regular visitor to the women's prison. Over the next several months Stacey learned to fully appreciate God's grace and forgiveness. She grew spiritually, and shared her faith in Christ with other inmates.

Chapter 2
Alcohol/Drug Addiction

The middle-age woman came into my office with her friend. "I can't take anymore of the abuse," she cried. "When he threatens the kids and me, and he walks around the house yelling and screaming, throwing things…I just can't take it." She wrapped the tissue around her fingers several times.

"How much does this go on?" I questioned.

"Whenever he's drinking."

"So what we need to do is to get him to stop drinking." I started to reach behind me for a folder where I kept information on Alcoholics Anonymous, Al-Anon, and other support groups.

"No, that's not it. I don't mind if he drinks as long as he doesn't act so mean." She sounded serious. Her friend looked surprised at the response, as I'm sure I did as well. "You see, he didn't get picked up for promotion when he thought he should three years ago, so he takes the pressure off by having a few drinks."

"But he's also mean to you and the kids when he drinks—you told me that." I could see where this was going, and I didn't like it.

"Well, yes. But if you could just get him to calm down when he drinks, and just not be mean to us—that would be alright with…"

I shook my head emphatically and held my hand up for her to stop talking. "Ma'am, I am not in the business of retraining alcoholics on how to behave when they are drunk. No one is. I'm not going to do it."

"Where else can I go?" she asked, surprised by my response. "He doesn't have to stop drinking, does he?"

"If you want his behavior to change, then yes, he does."

She thought for a moment. "How can I make him do that?"

"You can't. He has to want to. You can try and make him want to."

"How can I make him want to?"

That's when I reached for the folder again, this time handing information to her.

UNDERSTANDING THE CRISIS

First let's take a look at the American Medical Association's definition of alcoholism.

> **Alcoholism:** An illness that is characterized by
> significant impairment in the emotional, psychological,

spiritual, physical, and social areas that is directly associated with the persistent and excessive use of alcohol. Impairment may involve psychological or social dysfunction. Alcoholism also is manifested as a type of drug dependence of pathological extant and pattern, which ordinarily interferes seriously with the patient's mental and physical health and his adaptation to his environment.

There are many factors to consider when discussing alcoholism and drug addiction. First of all, in most areas of counseling and treatment, alcohol is considered a drug. Therefore, the treatment for the alcoholic involves a medical factor. The American Medical Association's definition illustrates the medical community's view of alcoholism as a drug dependency illness. Alcoholics Anonymous and Alcoholics Victorious, along with several other groups, have accepted and adopted the AMA definition. Alcoholism, in this case, is treated as a medical illness.

Non-medical community support providers, such as Alcohol Anonymous (AA), accept the AMA definition of alcoholism but take a different angle. Rather than provide counseling and a medical model, AA participants meet for the mutual support of one another using a twelve-step recovery program. In the program, participants who have been sober for a lengthy period of time sponsor new participants, and provide them with encouragement and support in their endeavor to become sober. AA teaches that though sober, they still consider themselves alcoholics.

There are several other programs built upon the AA's twelve-step model, some of which are: Narcotics Anonymous, Overeaters Anonymous, Alcoholics Victorious (similar to AA, but based on Evangelical Christian tenets), and others.

Which is better? It depends upon the individual circumstances. Some people need the medical treatment. Other people need the long term support which the fellowship of a group such as AA or NA offers, or some people may need both.

For one who has never been addicted to a substance, understanding the topic of addiction is difficult. Physically, not feeding the addiction creates problems for the addict's body. For alcoholics and some drug addicts, their body's shake, their muscles ache, headaches develop and increase, and they find it nearly impossible to function. Withdrawing from some drugs "cold turkey" (abruptly stopping drug use) can literally shut the body down.

Mentally, it is a bit more difficult to explain, as different drugs and alcohol cause different symptoms. But often a person's mind screams for the chemical it has become addicted to. I have sat with people who were hallucinating because they *weren't* getting the drug they had been using. At times the situation gets scary, and people have become violent.

Overall, the most important issue to consider when working with an addict is, their drug of choice *is* their coping mechanism. It is their method for checking out of reality, and not facing life's problems and difficult circumstances. This can be difficult for non-addicts to understand and accept. However, if you, the reader, are unwilling to accept that by getting drunk or high, the addict is "checking out of reality" temporarily to avoid coping with difficult situations, then you are destined to fail in your efforts to help get them off their addiction. Therein is where many people fail, and here is why:

> "John" comes home from work after a long day dealing with a difficult boss and unpleasant work circumstance. "Mary" meets him at the door with a load of bills in her hand, complaints about the kids acting up, and says her car is making a funny noise. John grabs a glass and bottle, pours himself a drink, and starts to relax. As the alcohol takes effect, a fog sets in, the mind begins to relax, and his and Mary's problems can wait. More to drink, more for fewer problems....

"Ashley" comes home from school, only to be met by mom and dad holding a discussion about her report card. As she puts her books down, statements of, "you're grounded until these grades come up," made by well-meaning parents hit her harder than she is willing to deal with at the moment. Soon the home is filled with yelling and screaming. Ashley darts out of the house and joins friends. One friend passes her a small pipe which she puffs, and soon her mind relaxes, and soon all of her problems aren't as real.

"John and Ashley" use their addictions to avoid coping with reality. And realistically, all of us use something or someone to cope with reality: aggressiveness, defense mechanisms, avoidance, suicide, food, etc. Other coping mechanisms such as prayer, teamwork, and facing issues head on, are more effective and much better for the body. Addicts have to be taught and trained in how to use effective coping mechanisms. That's where clinics and support groups come in. They help addicts learn to change their thinking and methods of coping, to change their perceptions of themselves, and to methodically deal with reality.

The weakness in the approach of some in church settings has been to treat alcohol and drug addicted people as sinners who choose not to repent and give up their sin. That is only part of the picture. Essentially, what the church needs to do is treat addiction as the illness that it is, yet, adopting the philosophy of Alcoholics Victorious Statement of Addiction and Recovery:

> Concerning the spiritual implications of alcoholism; we believe it has its roots in alienation from God and the violation of conscience. We accept the Biblical definition of "drunkenness" as a sin which prohibits those who practice it from entrance into the kingdom of God (Galatians 5:19–21; Romans 7:21). We believe that God's power is able to deliver individuals from the compulsion to drink, and to set them free from the emotional, psychological, social, spiritual, and physical consequences of an alcoholic lifestyle.

> Although an individual may be delivered from the compulsion to drink (and is no longer a "drunkard" in the spiritual sense), we recognize that he is still an alcoholic in the therapeutic sense. We believe the continued use of alcohol results in changes in the emotions, mind, and body that do not disappear upon an alcoholic's salvation. On a physiological level, he will always be "sensitized" to alcohol. Total abstinence, therefore, is a must; any use of alcohol can "activate"

the chemical mechanisms of addiction leading to compulsive drinking and behavior.

We believe this physical aspect of the disease of alcoholism will remain with the recovering alcoholic until he is glorified and receives his new body from the Lord. With the acknowledgement of this fact, the Christian alcoholic will be all the more diligent to abstain from drinking, recognizing the dire consequences of alcohol use. We further believe that, if he never drinks again, this physical aspect of the illness will have no other actual effect on his life and Christian walk.

We believe that professional counseling and therapy is usually necessary to help individuals to overcome the consequences of alcoholism. Also, we recognize that alcoholic's families need to be a part of the recovery process by receiving specialized help themselves. We accept the Twelve Steps of Alcoholics Anonymous as a reliable and orderly approach to recovery from alcoholism. We also believe that there are some very specific scriptural principles that must be applied to such an individual to assist him in a victorious and fruitful Christian walk.

In following Alcoholics Victorious' Statement of Addiction and Recovery, churches, and Christians individually, will be able to assist alcoholics and addicts recover.

APPLICABLE SCRIPTURE

Wine is a mocker and beer a brawler; whoever is led astray by them is not wise. —Proverbs 20:1

The acts of the sinful nature are obvious: ... drunkenness ... I warn you, as I did before, that those who live like this will not inherit the kingdom of God. —Galatians 5:19–21

Do not get drunk on wine, which leads to debauchery. Instead, be filled with the Spirit. —Ephesians 5:18

WHAT TO PRAY FOR

- Pray for the alcoholic or addict to be healed.

- Pray for the family of the alcoholic or addict.

- Pray for those providing treatment and support.

- Pray for God to reveal the spiritual needs of those you help.

HOW TO HELP

In order for you to help the alcoholic or drug addict *they must want to quit their addiction*. If they don't want to be sober or clean, you won't be able to help them. Prison employees and families of alcoholics and drug addicts can tell you that you can lock someone up behind bars for years, and it still doesn't take the addiction away. Only the desire on the part of the alcoholic or drug addict to be free from their addiction will actually enable you to help. The question then becomes, how do I help them to want to quit?

The first suggestion I have is to do some serious research on the support in your area. Find local treatment centers, hospitals with addiction clinics, recovery centers, and support groups such as Alcoholics Anonymous, Narcotics Anonymous, and Alcoholics Victorious. Talking with your pastor, a member of a support group, or your doctor, is an excellent place to start. If you have insurance, you may wish to call them to see what they recommend. Visit any facility you are thinking of using and ask questions so you can learn their program and procedures.

Second, I highly recommend you attend Al-Anon for support, education, and fellowship.

Next, plan and execute an intervention with family and friends of the alcoholic/addict. Include the spouse, parents, grandparents, siblings, children (depending upon their age and maturity), close friends, teachers, pastor, employer and/or fellow employees, neighbors, and anyone else who knows them and would have significant input.

In my experience, getting all the necessary people to the intervention won't be the problem, people want to come and be part of helping the alcoholic/addict try to recover. The problem is getting the alcoholic/addict to the intervention. If they are aware of the procedure, they very likely will balk at it and leave. Remember, they will be hearing their coping mechanism is being removed, they have to face reality, and they are going to endure withdrawal symptoms—not things they wish to face. However, in the interventions I have helped set up, we have had commanding officers order their personnel to attend. We performed them at a hospital bedside. Another time we had a police officer pickup and deliver a person to intervention (in a small town in Alaska, you can get a lot of interesting things done). Once we even told a man he was attending a party—the intervention was complete with balloons and streamers (big friends kept him there).

In many locations a treatment center will ask the members of the intervention to attend a planning meeting. They will go over the process with the team, and in some cases offer to attend. This service, if offered should be accepted.

The following are the key points for conducting an intervention:

1. There should be one designated person in charge of the intervention.

2. This person should be someone the alcoholic trusts and respects, who can keep control of the intervention, and who is able to tell when the alcoholic is being deceitful and call them on it.

3. The person in charge should be firm, direct, caring, and knowledgeable of the alcoholic/addict's past and present.

4. The person in charge should open the intervention by explaining to the alcoholic/ addict why everyone is there, including him/her.

5. One by one each person should then give their observations of the alcoholic/addict's behavior, how it affects them, and how it makes them feel.

6. The observations (#5) should be in writing and read to the addict.

7. Each person should then state that they are not going to tolerate the addict's behavior any longer.

8. After each person has spoken, the plan or plans should be presented to the alcoholic/addict.

9. Remember, the alcoholic/addict is most likely going to be defensive, angry, defiant, and very likely ready to walk out, if they haven't done so already.

10. Each person in the intervention group should remain firm in their conviction that they are there for the alcoholic/addict's best interest and the best interest of all concerned.

11. The plan should be ready to be implemented immediately—that day or evening if possible.

In one intervention I observed while stationed on Okinawa, the service members' wife had his bags packed and ready for him to be checked into treatment for alcoholism. It should be noted that her bags were packed as well, because if he had of refused treatment, she was going to leave him for good.

Be prepared to take the addict to treatment immediately after the intervention. During the time between the intervention and the entry into the treatment program chosen, the addicted person should be closely observed in the event they attempt to harm themselves or escape for a drink or fix. The person should not be allowed to drive to treatment alone; someone should drive them there.

The question arises, what should be done if the alcoholic/addict refuses treatment? My answer is that all support enabling them to continue their habit must stop. If they are arrested for DUI or possession of narcotics, they should not be bailed out, nor should money be provided for an attorney. Family should not allow themselves to be abused physically *or mentally and emotionally*. Employers should not accept tardiness, absenteeism, or arriving at work hung-over. In most of the situations I have seen where this plan has taken place, and the alcoholic/addict eventually relented and accepted treatment.

The alternative is to have alcoholic/addict legally committed to treatment by a court. The process and requirements for this vary from state to state. Therefore seek the advice of an attorney. Treatment centers are likely to have procedures for the court ordered treatment on file along with recommended attorneys.

There are other considerations when a juvenile is involved. Parents or guardians can have a child committed to a treatment against their will. State laws vary, but the process is generally easier than for an adult, and is considered in the best interest of the minor. An excellent referral for this is Teen Challenge, which has outstanding programs for youth treatment, as well as for adults. They have 150 treatment centers throughout the country, as well as 250 overseas, and they have an excellent Web site (www.teenchallenge.com).

The outcome after treatment, whether in-patient or through a support group such as Alcoholics Anonymous may be disconcerting. Everyone close to the alcoholic/addict will have to adjust to the "new" person, their new schedule of meetings, and generally being around them, as they adjust to a clean and sober life. Be prepared for this by listening to other people who have experienced it.

You or the person you are helping through this situation may want to contact New Life Ministries or similar organization for treatment in codependency recovery after living with an alcoholic/addict for a considerable period of time. (Paul Meier, founder of New Life Ministries, is co-author of *Love is a Choice*, the best written Christian book on codependency.) The national toll free number for New Life Ministries is: 1-800-NEW-LIFE or 1-800-639-5433.

For further information on conducting an intervention, I recommend the book LOVE FIRST: A Family's Guide to Intervention by Jeff Jay and Debra Jay.

Chapter 3
Computer Addiction

I stood thanking all the volunteers who helped paint and clean an elementary school in Thailand when a sailor, Linda, from another ship approached me. "I really need to talk to you, Chaplain."

"Let me clean up on my ship, and I'll meet you down on your mess deck. Can you give me an hour?"

She looked at her watch, "Okay Chaplain that will be fine."

An hour later I slid into a booth opposite Linda. "Sir, we've been gone for four months now. I just called home, and my husband hasn't registered for college, or even left the house to look for work."

"What has he been doing?"

"He's on the computer, sometimes twenty-four-hours a day. He got out of the Navy nearly three months before we left on deployment, and before I left he would be on Nintendo or the computer when I left for work, and then he'd be on when I got home."

"Does he do anything else?" I had heard of kids being on the computer too many hours, or an adult who worked using computers, but not of an adult playing computer games all day.

"Often, no," she shook her head slowly. "When I come in from working, he usually hasn't showered—sometimes he's eaten only one meal."

"What about errands?"

"No, I have to shop, do laundry, all that."

"Have you spoken to his family?" I questioned.

"Yes, I called them while you were cleaning up. It has them concerned too." She took a deep breath. "He was going to go back to Colorado and visit them while I was gone. Now we are six weeks from returning to San Diego, and he has no plans to go visit. What should I do?"

I thought for several moments. "Until you return to San Diego, there isn't much you can do, except encourage him to seek help. He can start with a doctor, chaplain, or Family Service Center counselor." I paused to let that sink in. "It might help if anyone from his family would go out and help him seek counseling."

"I asked my mother-in-law about that. She's as concerned as I am." She shook her head slowly and tears formed in her eyes. "What causes something like this to happen?"

UNDERSTANDING THE CRISIS

Computers aren't inherently evil. Just as James 3:9–10 talks of the good and evil uses of the tongue, we need to understand that there are good and evil uses for the computer, especially when connected to the Internet.

I consulted a friend of mine, Judy Hessler, a Behavior Intervention Specialist, in researching the topic of computer addiction. Judy was able to give me insight into this phenomenon.

People who sit in front of the computer for hours every day, in non-working situations, generally are avoiding reality. The computer, whether used for games, chatting, porn, music, or something else, helps them escape from events, tasks, or unpleasant memories and feelings such as inadequacy, pain, shame, and others. By escaping, they don't have to face reality.

Computer addiction is not the same as a chemical addiction such as alcohol or drugs (see chapter 17). The body does not go through a physiological withdrawal, causing a physical reaction like the loss of a drug. However, where some people have compared it to TV addiction, the computer is much easier to escape with because it doesn't have commercials, or other breaks when programming changes. The computer game, chat session, or program can continue for hours on end without a break, controlled by the gamer, player, or addict.

In my own experiences in counseling people addicted to computers, or similar non-chemical addictions, I have noticed a difference in patterns for men and women.

Men tend to feel insecure in themselves, and use the computer to escape feelings of inadequacy about themselves as men, husbands, and fathers. Generally, they come from single parent homes, or where their father wasn't present, and he had addictions which weren't dealt with properly.

Women tend to be insecure in their relationships as well as in themselves.

However, where women get trapped on the computer is not so much in the games as it is in the chat rooms. They often develop relationships with people on-line. A major concern with this situation, beyond the time spent, is that often boundaries are not set, and warning bells don't sound when a predatory relationship develops.

If the computer is withdrawn, there is a void in the user's mind, and life, which unless filled with something beneficial, is likely to revert to a similar addiction. Simply removing them from the computer does not turn them into a well-adjusted person. In order to truly help someone addicted to the computer, you have to address the underlying issue, such as what they are avoiding or trying to block out of their minds while they spend hours each day in front of the monitor. [Note: This situation is quite different than Case #2 in chapter 14, Job Loss]

APPLICABLE SCRIPTURE

Of course there are no biblical references to the use of the computer. There are, however, references to what one does with his or her time.

> Finally, brothers, whatever is true, whatever is noble, whatever is right, whatever is pure, whatever is lovely, whatever is admirable—if anything is excellent or praiseworthy—think about such things. Whatever you have learned or received, or heard from me, or seen in me—put into practice. And the God of peace will be with you.
>
> –Philippians 4:8–9

WHAT TO PRAY FOR

- Pray for the computer addict.
- Pray for the family of the computer addict.
- Pray for the counselor (you perhaps) helping the computer addict overcome his/her addiction.

HOW TO HELP

More than any of the other type of addiction, this is one area where I believe a layperson can truly help an addict. My reasoning is threefold:

1. A layperson, through a gentle, loving, caring presence may be able to "touch" the sore spot in the addict's mind and help them overcome it.
2. A layperson can help fill the void in the addict's life when they draw away from the computer.
3. A layperson can be a daily or near daily presence in the addict's life, at least for a while, whereas a counselor most likely cannot be.

I must caution you against going in like the cavalry with the intent of rescuing or fixing the computer addict. First and foremost you must develop a relationship with the person, looking at them through the eyes of Jesus, just as Jesus looked at people before he healed them. You are positioning yourself more as a coach than a counselor.

Secondly, have in mind the intent to mentor them. Mentoring is the manner you will use to replace the time and "brain energy" they used on the computer with something beneficial. Besides your Bible, I would recommend you have the following books:

Love is a Choice Hemfelt, Minirth, and Meier; Thomas
Nelson Publishers

Telling Yourselves the Truth Backus and Chapman;
Bethany House Publishers

Changes That Heal Henry Cloud; Zondervan

The Worth of a Man Dave Dravecky; Zondervan (for men)

The first three books would be excellent for a man or woman. All
three are quite easy to read and understand, and can be used in a one-
on-one setting for developing a relationship, as well as discipleship. All
three books are compatible with the others.

When working with addicts, it is highly important to emphasize to
them that they are not "losers," "failures," or any other term. Most of
my experience is in working with depressed individuals and there is a
strong connection between depression and addiction.

In the military setting I use the rank structure as a metaphor, stating something to the effect, "At this point you're a recruit, but we will
soon move you up to Petty Officer, then to Chief ..."

In the event that the above doesn't work, or doesn't work as well as
you feel it should have, there are options you should consider.

If the family member or friend is still a student, you could ask that
the school psychologist look into their behavior.

If the family member or friend is an adult, the family and friends may choose to hold an intervention, much the same way I suggested in the chapter on eating disorders and alcohol/drug addictions. While computer addiction may not ruin a person's physical health, if anxieties or fears of inadequacies cause the addiction, the person needs to have counseling or therapy, or be willing to accept the layperson mentoring previously suggested.

Chapter 4
Depression: Including Bipolar Disorder

I had thoughts of Chinese food on my mind as I headed towards the outer door to our office, when a young sailor approached me.

"I need to talk to you right away," he said desperation filling his face.

"Sure, let's go in my office." We entered my office and I put some music on to mask our voices. Taking my jacket off I asked him, "What can I do for you?"

"It's my wife. She's taken a turn for the worse."

"How do you mean?" I had never met the sailor's wife, nor talked to him about her.

"She began acting strangely shortly before I deployed." He began wringing and releasing his hands. "Lately, with another deployment coming up she often doesn't get out of bed till nearly noon. Sometimes our daughter doesn't get out the door for the school bus, and our two-year-old son isn't fed until she gets up." He took his cover (hat in Navy parlance) off and rolled it in his hands. "I'm afraid the state is going to get called in for child neglect."

I nodded slowly. "You mean in addition to the concern you have for your wife and kids."

"Oh yes, that's what I meant." He seemed relieved I understood where he was coming from. "Anyway, Sir, my Chief sent me here to see you."

"How long has she actually been like this? You mentioned a deployment period."

"I think it's been a little over two years."

"And you have a two-year-old son?"

"Yes, he was born right before I deployed."

I sat and calculated the time in my head. "So she had a double whammy...pregnancy and loneliness with you gone. And then you can throw in postpartum depression on top of that."

"I...I don't really know anything about that." He looked confused.

"Was she like that with her first pregnancy and soon after?"

"I don't know. I didn't know her then."

"Do you think she'd be willing to come and talk to me?"

"I don't know. She might. She does know something is wrong, she just doesn't know what."

UNDERSTANDING THE CRISIS

What I am not going to do is give medical/clinical definitions of depression, to the point of having readers trying to diagnose and treat people who may or may not be depressed. That could end up being a risky situation. I will stick with layman's terms, situations, and signs.

The first thing I want you to understand is that there are multiple types of depression, and multiple causes. Some people can be short term or long term depressed due to circumstances, such as in the case of the death of a loved one, job loss, financial difficulties, or many other situations. When those events occur, expectations aren't met, and depression results.

Normally, when a significant period of time passes (as in the death of a loved one), or the situation is remedied, such as in the financial crunch time, their depression will lighten or be alleviated. Counseling would be a good thing, but love, friendship, and support of friends, family, and church generally work well.

Long term depression, simplified, may be caused by circumstances, as in the death of a loved one, especially (from my experience counseling) a spouse or child. Divorce when it involves a long marriage seems to be the most common cause from my observations. There are other causes, mainly involving family, abortion, work circumstances, incarceration, loneliness, and more.

One cause of depression, where I have had quite a bit of success counseling, is "sin caused" depression. This is where a person was raised a Christian and *knows* what is right and what is sinful. Yet, despite their knowledge, they choose to sin. Once we begin counseling and determine this is the root cause of their sin, the rest is easy *if* they're willing to repent and ask for forgiveness. That's a big *if* though.

Depression also has roots in a person's outlook at life in general. If all they have known is suffering emotionally, physically, or both, it is an emotional outlook so common to them that they are comfortable with it. Even after things change for the better for them, they seem morose, typically thinking that things are going to return to the negative for them.

Beware of the trap. There is a pitfall or a trap if you prefer that term, that goodhearted people often fall into when working with depressed people. This is a huge trap for pastors. The trap is in helping people who use depression as a manipulative tool. If a person acts depressed and helpless, people often jump in and do things for them. Manipulative people learn how to work this to their advantage, and people often don't see themselves as being used. This easily becomes a time/labor/money trap that, for some, never seems to end. It can go on for years, and I have seen it done so.

Clearly, there are depressed people and they need our help. I am not referring to them at all when discussing "the trap," Rather, I am addressing the abusers, who have no reservations in having others do things for them, which they could actually do for themselves, and they accomplish this by acting depressed and helpless. Goodhearted people—acting out of love—can become enablers if they are unaware of this trap.

Truthfully, I have been caught in this trap, and it was the experience and wisdom of an older pastor who pointed out to me what was actually occurring. Once I gently confronted the person, the next time he attempted using me, and gently but firmly said, "Enough," he moved on to using someone else. Eventually, he packed up and moved to another community.

Some common signs of depression are:

- Listlessness/helplessness
- Constant or near constant exhaustion
- Lack of interest in normal hobby activities
- Lack of personal care
- Over eating or eating very little
- Thoughts of suicide
- Easily confused
- Easily forgetting things
- Abuse of alcohol or drugs
- Hypochondria/seeking medical care for non-existent or very minor ailments

- Lack of concern about work or school

- Withdrawn or desire for solitude

- Lack of or no interest in sex

- Gloomy outlook

- Bitterness/unforgiveness

- Feeling overwhelmed

People exhibiting any number of these signs, especially thoughts of suicide, should seek or be directed to professional help. If the person will not seek professional help, get professional help for them in the form of a pastoral visit, a visiting nurse, a county mental health call. It should be arranged especially if the person has children.

Someone talking of suicide, even if they aren't using the word "suicide," should have immediate medical attention called to them.

The other circumstance where long term depression is involved is due to a medical condition. Simplified, the brain chemistry is out of normal operating levels. Examples of this would be hormone levels during pregnancy or postpartum. Another cause would be the neurotransmitters (synapses) in the brain aren't firing properly.

The bipolar individual will have periods of "highs" where they appear happy, cheerful, or perhaps what one would call "normal." Then the bipolar individual will go into a period of depression. This is a medical condition. The bipolar individual generally doesn't recognize their emotional states, has no warning when their emotional state is changing, and tends to believe his/her actions are normal. I personally have had no success at counseling bipolar individuals, nor do I know any psychologists, counselors, therapists, or other persons in ministry who have had success at counseling bipolar diagnosed individuals.

Medical attention is warranted in bipolar cases. However, family members of bipolar sufferers often need support, especially if the bipolar individual refuses to take their medication, or take themselves off their medication. They often, without warning, can go from a euphoric high to an intense depression or from an extreme low to a manic high. I have had family members tell me it's a life of climbing peaks and sliding into valleys, or a life of roller-coaster rides.

Medications for bipolar sufferers smooth out the peaks and valleys, and makes life more bearable for everyone around them, including the bipolar individual. Bipolar individuals have told me that had they known how much easier their life would be on medication, they would have jumped at the opportunity to get on the medication at the first hint or offer.

In living or working with a bipolar person, you must remember that this is an illness, and not something they are choosing to have. Give them praise encouragement for seeking out medical help and treatment, and give them praise and encouragement for continuing the treatment. Going on a lifetime of the medication regimen is not easy, especially when the bipolar person doesn't see the results of the bipolar condition, nor do they generally see the results of the treatment. But they do hear and feel the support they receive for going on and continuing treatment.

APPLICABLE SCRIPTURE

[Does not apply to medically caused depression]

For day and night your hand was heavy upon me; my strength was sapped as in the heat of summer. Then I acknowledged my sin to you and did not cover my iniquity. I said, "I will confess my transgressions to the LORD"—and you forgave the guilt of my sin.

Therefore let everyone who I'd godly pray to you while you may be found; surely when the mighty waters rise, they will not reach him. You are my hiding place; you will protect me from trouble and surround me with songs of deliverance.

—Psalm 32:4–7

An anxious heart weighs a man down, but a kind word cheers him up.

—Proverbs 12:25

A happy heart makes the face cheerful, but heartache crushes the spirit.

—Proverbs 15:13

"The most important one," answered Jesus, "is this: 'Hear, O Israel, the Lord our God, the Lord is one. Love the Lord your God with all of your heart and with all of your soul and with all of your mind and with all of your strength."

—Mark 12:29–30

Peace I leave with you; my peace I give you. I do not give as the world gives. Do not let your hearts be troubled and do not be afraid.

—John 14:27

WHAT TO PRAY FOR

- Pray for patience.
- Pray for healing for the depressed person.
- Pray for the family of the depressed person.
- If the depression is a medical situation, pray for the treating physician(s).

- If the depression is sin caused, pray the person will repent and seek forgiveness.

HOW TO HELP

Counseling people who have been depressed for long periods of time where the cause isn't medical, is time consuming, tiring, and at times—frustrating work. Yet, if successful, it is highly rewarding. It is even more rewarding where the depressed person has a family that has been highly affected by the depression, and you see the burden lifted from the entire family.

My first recommendation for helping someone who is depressed is to assess the cause of the depression and the possibility of suicide. If it is due to a specific cause, loss of their job for example, then unless the person is advanced in years, it most likely will be short-term depression. That is, as long as the person hasn't suffered long-term depression in the past.

The initial care for helping a depressed person (not caused by a medical condition) is careful listening. Often, when helping a person with short-term depression you will find they need to talk to someone who is willing to listen. You are likely to hear some anger, bitterness, frustration, confusion, and perhaps a bit of grieving. This is generally frustration of their expectations not being met. After allowing a person to unload verbally you will see their countenance change. Just unloading helps them more than you will realize. There have been many times when someone has come to me for counseling and all I did was listen. Afterwards they would often say, "Hey, I feel better already."

After listening, if they still need help, zero in on what the specific need. If there are multiple causes, such as loneliness and finances, address each cause separately, and help them work through each as a separate issue. I would encourage you to assist them, but I would discourage you from taking over duties or responsibilities that would make them dependant on you or cause you to be an enabler. If you do, then the next time they are overwhelmed by circumstances, they will be more likely to return to depression rather than work through their circumstances.

If the depression is caused by sin, you have the option of leading the person to salvation, or to restoration. Ideally they will readily accept this. If, however, they turn you down, remember, they aren't turning you down so much as they are turning Jesus down. It hurts to see people do this, but it is their choice.

If they do accept salvation or restoration, don't stop there. This is a great place to begin discipling them. We are called to make disciples (Matthew 28:19–20).

If you find yourself going beyond a level at which you feel comfortable, seek help for yourself and for the depressed person. I highly recommend keeping your pastor informed of what you're involved in from the beginning.

At some point, should this become a long-term situation, you may turn the depressed person over to your pastor's care and counsel. Knowing what has been done will greatly benefit your pastor. Since it can be tiring and frustrating work, having your pastor's counsel and encouragement will benefit you.

If the situation appears to be long-term depression, immediately refer the person for professional counseling. Many pastors, recognizing their own limitations, choose to refer long-term depressed individuals to counselors, psychologists, or therapists. Pastors who do this should not be criticized or looked down on.

Long-term depressed individuals need specialized care, and in some cases, medication to help overcome their depression. Often their depression has been passed down from a parent, or is a result of child-hood abuse, and depression is all they have ever known. Clinicians who work with depressed individuals will often bring in family members to help overcome the depression, and may choose to put the depressed person in group therapy, something pastors generally aren't able to do.

If the depression is caused by a medical condition, a counselor, therapist, psychologist, or family practice physician will probably rec-ognize this rather quickly. They will know a medical specialist (usually a psychiatrist, though laws vary from state to state) to refer the depressed individual to for further treatment, though they may choose to treat the depressed individual as a team. This would also be true for people with bipolar disorder.

If you find yourself working within "the trap" I mentioned in the explanation, helping someone you believe is using depression as a manipulative tool, the best way to handle that situation is to break the chain. Gentle direct questions to the individual, such as, "Why can't you do that?" or "Why haven't you done something to correct that situation?" puts the person in the position of answering for their behavior.

In working to break the chain of manipulative behavior you are likely to be called names and accused of being heartless and cold. Sure this hurts, and certainly you aren't going to like it. The fact is if you don't break the chain, you will be stuck being an enabler, and the manipulator will not change.

One final suggestion is to perform a family intervention for someone who will not seek treatment for his or her depression. Depressed people don't generally know the extent of their depression or the ramifications it has on family members, friends, neighbors, fellow students, co-workers, and others. A loving, caring, helpful group may be able to explain it to them. I have heard of this being done and it proved to be successful. I would refer you to the pattern I set forth in the chapter on eating disorders.

FOLLOW UP

The sailor's wife needed medical treatment for her postpartum depression. Some other wives from the ship stepped in to help with childcare, ensuring the oldest child was sent off to school in time. She was put on a mild anti-depressant prescription, which helped her overcome her postpartum depression.

Chapter 5
Eating Disorders

I was still new to ministry when Liz, a single woman in the church, approached me. "I am entering the eating disorders program at Eastside Hospital tomorrow. I want to make sure you, and others from the church, come visit me." I must have looked stunned, for she continued, "You aren't the only one who is surprised. None of my friends, and no one here at the church knew anything of what's been going on."

"So you were able to hide it well." I observed.

"Oh yes, from everyone except my mom and sister. They both caught me purging."

Liz was in her mid-twenties, highly energetic, and polite. Though energetic, she was somewhat shy, and had low self-esteem. Everyone in the singles group liked Liz, which she seemed unwilling to understand.

"How long is the program at Eastside?"

"It's a full month. I can't leave during that time. But I can have family and pastoral visits during the first two weeks."

After Liz had been in the Eating Disorders program a week, my wife and I paid a visit to Liz. The visiting area had a large glass window enabling the nursing staff to observe, but not listen, to the visit. Later when I would work in the prison setting as a chaplain, I would reflect on this "observing" atmosphere.

"Liz, you look a little down. Is the program not working for you?" I inquired.

"I thought about leaving this past weekend. We have no control. We're watched and monitored all the time." She sounded very frustrated. "Everything we do is evaluated and recorded. And the group meetings are brutal at times. I'm not used to that much honesty."

"But you stayed."

"Yeah, I guess I did." She sighed in frustration. "I know I can't spend the rest of my life binging and purging." Liz was fidgeting nervously. "And I am learning. I know that my bulimia was caused by how I felt about myself rather than being about food."

"Is the program working for you then?" I asked.

Liz nodded, "It is. And it's keeping me from purging, so I guess the lack of privacy is working. Once I get over the control issues it will work better."

"I think there's something else too, isn't there?"

Liz thought for a moment, and then smiled. "And once I feel better about myself, too."

UNDERSTANDING THE CRISIS

Eating disorders are on the rise. While affecting mostly women, men, generally in the overeating category, are starting to be diagnosed with eating disorders as well. The three main categories of eating disorders are: anorexia, bulimia, and overeating.

Anorexia: Women with anorexia have a fear of gaining weight and losing control, thus deny themselves food and hydration. They exercise, cook for others, and generally will not eat in public. They have a distorted view of their body shape, believing themselves to be larger and heavier than they are, even though they are thinner than average for their height. They will deny their symptoms and vigorously resist help.

Do: As a friend or family member, watch for lack of eating, concern about weight, and possibly possession of diet aids.

Bulimia: Women with bulimia will eat large amounts of food over a short period of time (binge), and then force themselves to vomit (purge). They tend to be heavy users of laxatives and diuretics. Bulimics feel out of control in their binges and purges. Bulimics generally have serious dental problems, as well as upper gastro-intestinal problems from their purges.

Do: As a family member or friend, watch for signs of purging after meals, as well as use of laxatives and diuretics.

Overeating: While being overweight may be the result of enjoying food, for purposes of this chapter I am referring to people who eat as a result of depression, low self-esteem, nervousness, or otherwise attempt to use food to cope with emotional problems. When stressed, these people binge eat, using food, rather than people, for comfort. Do not confuse this with gluttony. People in this category use food to cope the way an alcoholic uses liquor or a drug addict uses narcotics.

Do: As a family member or friend, watch for binge eating during stressful periods.

Eating disorders tend to begin in the teens. Alarmingly, anorexia is being diagnosed in young girls, as early as twelve and thirteen-years-old. Bulimia is being seen more and more on college campuses, which may be the result of competition for grades and popularity. My own observations show people with eating disorders tend to be:

- girls/women in late teens to early thirties
- come from highly critical parents with high expectations and low tolerance
- live in denial
- are above average at school or work

Many family members and close friends of people with eating disorders make the mistake (in good faith) of telling an anorexic to eat, a bulimic to stop throwing-up, and an overeater to diet, and think they are doing the person a service. While their intentions are good, often they are adding to the emotional stress the person is already carrying. The well-intentioned person needs to understand that an eating disorder, for anorexics and bulimics, is a form of control. It is a psychological and emotional illness. Thus, this requires expert help and treatment.

The person with an eating disorder needs to have their emotional, as well as their spiritual, views of themselves and their world changed. They need to have their system of coping changed as well. In other words, they need a serious lifestyle change, just as an alcoholic or a drug addict would. This generally involves professional long term care, which will be discussed in Procedures.

Lonnie V. Scott

APPLICABLE SCRIPTURE

For emotional stress/coping:

Do not be anxious about anything, but in everything,

by prayer and petition,

with thanksgiving, present your requests to God. And

the peace of God,

which transcends all understanding, will guard your

hearts and your minds in Christ Jesus.

Finally … whatever is true, whatever is noble, whatever

is right, whatever is pure, whatever is lovely, whatever is

admirable—if anything is excellent or praiseworthy—

think about such things. Whatever you have learned

or received … put into practice. And the God of peace

will be with you.

—Philippians 4:6–9

For control issues:

It is for freedom that Christ set us free. Stand firm,

then, and do not let yourselves be burdened again by a

yoke of slavery.

—Galatians 5:1

For self concept/personal value:

How great is the love the Father has lavished on us,
that we should be called the children of God! And that
is what we are!

—1 John 3:1a

For life style change:

Be imitators of God, therefore, as dearly loved children
and live a life of love, just as Christ loved us and gave
himself up for us as a fragrant offering and sacrifice to
God. Live as children of the light (for the fruit of the
light consists in all goodness, righteousness and truth)
and find out what pleases the Lord.

—Ephesians 5:1, 8b–10

WHAT TO PRAY FOR

- Pray for a successful family/friend intervention.
- Pray for guidance in selecting an excellent recovery program.
- Pray for your friend/family member will listen.
- Pray for the physical, spiritual, and emotional health of your friend/family member.
- Pray for the counselor(s) treating your friend/family member.

HOW TO HELP

Convincing someone to enter treatment for an eating disorder is extremely difficult. Most people with an eating disorder will vigorously deny they have one (even though they know they have one), and therefore consider treatment unnecessary. Even when confronted with evidence (lost weight, diet aids, caught in the act of forced vomiting), they will excuse it away. Many of the instances of treatment of anorexia I have been made aware of began in the emergency room when the patient collapsed. From the emergency room they were transferred to another ward, and then referred for treatment.

Many referrals for eating disorders do come from primary care physicians when the patient is seen for other reasons. I know of cases where a physician diagnosed bulimia from examining the mouth and throat of patients and confronted the patient with his suspicions. From there he referred the women for further treatment.

Overeating is probably the easiest to diagnose and refer or consult. While attempting to be supportive, I recommend against simply referring a person to a self-help diet program, or that they purchase a diet aid from a store or TV commercial. The overeater needs to be in a supportive program to help improve their emotional well-being.

In giving steps to follow, first I'd like to mention some "what not to do" procedures. These are very important in helping the person with an eating disorder:

1. Don't act out of your frustration. Instances of this might be saying something to the affect of, "Alright, go ahead and starve/ eat yourself to death. See if I care."

2. Do not attempt to force the anorexic/bulimic to eat or the overeater to diet. This very likely will drive them away. The emotional pressure on them is often enormous, and your efforts may have the opposite effect. The only place force works is in a treatment facility.

3. Lastly, don't quit. This truly is a ministry. Your prayers, your encouragement, your faith, and your love are a necessary part of the family member's/friend's recovery.

There are two methods I will recommend for getting your friend/ family member into recovery. Both have a high success rate, and both are generally covered by insurance.

The first is direct medical intervention. This involves the friend/ family member being screened by a physician. If the appointment (other than through the emergency room) were for another reason, then it would be wise, and ethical, to alert the physician of the friend family/member's eating disorder.

The alternate method is to hold a family/friend intervention meeting. This would involve gaining the support of people close to the person with the eating disorder. Besides family and friends, you may want to have the person's minister, coworker, and if a student, a teacher. Try not to overwhelm the person with numbers, five to seven people will be sufficient. With the person present, each family member presents what he or she has observed the person doing, and how he or she sees the actions affecting him or her. Each person present should also affirm their support for the friend/family member should they agree to treatment.

Don't expect the person with the eating disorder to sit quietly in agreement. Generally they will rationalize their behavior. However, if they do listen, and agree to treatment, which often happens, have a plan in place. Praise their agreement and pledge your support.

Developing a plan often depends upon where you or the person with the eating disorder lives. It may also depend on what insurance or other financial resources you have. You may also need to check into what the state or county offers. If military or veteran, check into what the local military or VA hospital offers.

Mental health professionals, pastors, physicians, and social workers are resources for referrals to treatment centers. I would also check the Internet and the yellow pages. Also highly recommended would be to call to a nationally known chain of clinics such as the Minirth-Meier/New Life Clinics. If there is a New Life Clinic near you they will refer you to it. Their clinics have a very high success rate. Visit the treatment facility if you are able. Seek out what books, videos, or other materials they utilize or recommend and, if you can, obtain them for yourself. If you are able to visit the facility, explain that you are seeking to place your friend/family member into treatment, and ask for their recommendation.

All participants at the intervention should understand what the plan is, and hopefully, be in agreement with it. Working as a team is vitally important in this setting. Explain to the participants that you visited the facility (if you conducted a visit), and explain the program. Their knowledge of the program may be useful during the intervention.

When conducting the intervention, there are some simple ground rules I recommend following:

1. Allow only one person to speak at a time, to include the person with the eating disorder.

2. Present facts ("I've seen you throwing up several times lately.") and how the situation is affecting you, as well as them.

3. Let the person know you are acting out of love and concern.

4. Minimize or alleviate outside interruptions. Take the telephone off the hook, turn off cell phones. Don't provide snacks. Focus on the intervention.

5. Be firm. Don't allow the person to rationalize away facts.

6. If the person with the eating disorder doesn't agree to your plan, ask them for an alternative. The group should listen to the alternative plan, but should consider it seriously *only if* they consider it as good as the one they have already supported.

7. Remember that the eating disorder is about control.

8. Remember, you are not putting the person on trial, and you are not attorneys. You aren't seeking a conviction. While being firm, remain loving and supportive.

Hopefully the intervention will work. However, the person with the eating disorder may choose not to listen or agree to treatment. They may get up and walk out. Let them (if they are an adult).

If the person is a minor, as parents you may have legal options for placing the minor in treatment. You will need to check with a legal advisor, your medical advisor, your insurance company, and the clinic in order to determine what course to follow.

If the person is an adult, it may be that you have exercised all of your options until the person changes his/her mind, or until medical intervention becomes necessary to save the person's life.

Often clinics have strict visitation policies. Prior to making a visit familiarize yourself with their rules. Many clinics do not allow visits for the first week or two weeks so as to allow the patient to focus on the program. They probably have strict phone call policies as well. Be in agreement with the clinic on this. They have experience, they know what works.

Towards the end of the treatment, many programs ask for family and friends to participate. Do your best to do this, even if it involves taking time off work or traveling. It will mean a great deal to the patient and it will show your support.

Chapter 6
Miscarriage

The phone in my office rang as I was preparing to go PT (Navy parlance for physical training). The base chaplains' office advised me a very distraught woman was there needing to see a chaplain but their chaplains were all out of the office. I asked them to send the lady up to me.

A short time later, Tracy entered my office, sank onto my couch, and began to cry her heart out. She cried for nearly half-an-hour before she was able to tell me what the situation was.

"My husband is out to sea. We learned seven weeks ago that I was pregnant with our first child." She paused to wipe her eyes. "A month ago he left for deployment. I'm also active duty. I began experiencing severe cramps and a fever a few days ago. I went to the emergency room three days ago and the symptoms went away. I didn't notify Jason since it would stress him." She paused and took more tissue. "My mother arrived from back home to help take care of me, so my doctor released me. Two days ago I lost the baby."

At that point, Tracy chose to have her husband notified about the miscarriage.

Tracy and her husband, Jason, who had to remain at sea, believed the miscarriage to be the death of a baby. Tracy's mother, however, thought of the miscarriage as a pregnancy gone badly, and did not view the circumstances as anything but a medical problem.

Tracy's mother made statements such as, "It wasn't really a baby, it wasn't born yet," and "you're still young, you can have other babies."

Tracy was devastated by her mother's insensitivity to her loss and grief.

UNDERSTANDING THE CRISIS

There are differing views on what a miscarriage (also called a spontaneous abortion) represents. To many it means the death of a child, often a long-awaited child for couples who married late, or who had difficulty conceiving. Often the mother blames herself for causing the miscarriage due to over-work, stress, or physical activity. Therefore, guilt enters the picture. Sometimes the father takes on guilt as well for not doing more things around the house, causing his wife to have to do them and thus, in his mind, causing the miscarriage. I have seen many cases where the couple believes the miscarriage to be a form of punishment, sometimes from God.

A secondary problem is when the mother feels that she is inadequate as a woman to conceive and carry to full-term. Depression follows and has to be worked through to restore the woman to emotional and spiritual health.

Others, such as Tracy's mother, hold the belief that the miscarriage was not of a baby but of a fetus, which until birth, is not really a person. To those who hold this, a natural medical, though regretful, process occurred. In this case, guilt or serious grief is seldom encountered.

APPLICABLE SCRIPTURE

While no cases of miscarriage occur in the Bible, there are several cases of women grieving over being barren for long periods of time. Sarah was distressed so much over being barren that she asked Abraham to bear a child with her maidservant (Genesis 16). Rachel was so distressed and jealous at being barren while she watched her sister, Leah, bear children that she declared to her husband, Jacob, in Genesis 30:1, "Give me children, or I'll die!" Later, in the same chapter, she did the same thing as Sarah, giving her servant to her husband to bear children. Hannah declared herself to be in misery over the state of being barren, and her anguish caused Eli the priest to think she was drunk (1 Samuel 1:1–16).

WHAT TO PRAY FOR

- Pray that your presence will be a comfort to the parents.
- Pray for God's guidance in how to minister to the parents, and to others involved.
- Pray for the physical and emotional healing for the mother.
- Pray for strength for the couple to endure.

HOW TO HELP

It doesn't matter whether you believe the miscarriage was the death of a child or a medical mishap. If you want to be of help to the couple, or in Tracy's case with the absence of her husband, to the mother, the first step is to "just be there." As in Tracy's case, someone close caused her to feel further anguish due to trying to force her beliefs on Tracy. Your ministry of presence and listening will greatly help the parent(s).

The couple may choose to hold a funeral or memorial service, and you may support them, especially if they don't attend a church and need your advice.

You may also direct the parent(s) to resources (support groups, Web sites, counseling) if they seem open to it. Try not to appear as though you are pushing them away from yourself and on to someone else.

You may provide a "helping" ministry through cooking, cleaning, yard work, driving, etc. If, however, the parents decline, please abide by their wishes.

Certainly cards and flowers are appropriate.

Chapter 7
PTSD: Post Traumatic Stress Disorder

TERRI'S STORY

As I strolled about the prison camp's yard an unfamiliar voice called to me. Terri and Trina , two of the women inmates jogged toward me. I recognized one; she attended a codependency recovery group I held weekly at the chapel. The other, a woman about twenty-seven years old, I had seen but never spoken to. While the first woman, Trina, stopped about ten feet away. Terri approached me slowly, twice looking over her shoulder at her friend. She stopped two feet in front of me.

"Hi Chaplain Scott. Trina said I should talk to you."

"Let's go sit in the shade of that tree," I said pointing at the curb in an abundance of shade. "Here we'll be away from the interruption of my phone."

We sat on the curb, with Terri tucking her knees under her chin and me unbuttoning my suit jacket. She had a serious but casual demeanor. Trina hovered about a dozen feet away.

"I don't know where to start," Terri said. I stayed quiet allowing her to choose the beginning point. "I guess it all started when I was raped when I was sixteen…."

I listened as Terri poured her heart out.

THE OFFICE PICNIC TRAGEDY

Sirens sounded outside my Navy office. I looked out the window and saw fire engines and base police cars blocking the road around the ball field. This meant a med-evac was going to take place. Usually this was done for a civilian shipyard worker hurt on the job. Soon the small orange and white helicopter landed and a gurney was loaded, and the helicopter lifted off. As I sat down at my desk Petty Officer Roberts charged into my office.

"Chaps, Commander Marshall is on the phone, she says it's an emergency."

I picked up the handset and punched the flashing light. "Chaplain Scott."

CDR Marshall's voice sounded urgent. "Did you hear about the car accident involving Petty Officer Mendoza's child?" CDR Marshall was always calm and compassionate. Cutting to the chase was unlike her.

"No, Ma'am, I haven't heard," I said as I saw the last of the emergency vehicles driving away.

"One of the offices was having an outdoor luncheon. Petty Officer Evans was leaving to pick up some more chips and soda, and Petty Officer Mendoza's two-year-old daughter ran behind her car. Petty Officer Evans backed over the child—looks like she has a concussion. She is being flown to Children's Hospital."

"I'm on my way there now," I said as I grabbed my hat.

[Three hours later]

The phone rang twice and was answered. "CDR Marshall speaking"

"Chaplain Scott here. Petty Officer Austin and I are on our way back now. The baby and parents are doing fairly well. I will be coming back tomorrow."

"Thanks Chaplain. I'm sure they will appreciate it." CDR Marshall sounded relieved.

"Ma'am, we have to do a CISM [Critical Incident Stress Debriefing]. This was a serious injury to a child."

"Chaplain, this is Friday evening. We won't be able to get everyone over the weekend. I can call the Counseling and Advocacy Program Director, and we can meet Monday morning."

"Let's do it. I'll be one of the team members," I said. We had to do it as soon as possible. Caught up in the stress of the action, no one had told everyone present at the accident to return the next day.

Monday morning I met Donna and Carl, two civilian Navy counselors, and we walked to the office where Petty Officer Mendoza's co-workers were gathered. Donna, the clinic's director, started off.

"I'm Donna, and this is Carl. We're from the CAPS Center. You already know Chaplain Scott. We're here to help walk you through a Critical Incident Stress Debriefing. This will help you overcome the stress and anxiety of what you witnessed last Friday afternoon."

I carefully watched the twelve faces in the room. Some looked exhausted, like they hadn't slept all weekend.

UNDERSTANDING THE CRISIS

When people experience a traumatic event they will often experience mental/emotional and physical problems for a period afterwards. Some of the mental and emotional problems might be flashbacks, anxiety, anger, feelings the event is going to happen again, and lack of concentration. These are just some of the mental and emotional reactions.

Often a sight, sound, or smell will trigger a reaction. Untreated, this may go on for years.

Many physical reactions may arise. Some are: sleep problems, easily agitated by loud noises or startling events, heavy rapid heartbeat, and sweating.

Untreated, PTSD can lead to alcoholism, drug abuse, isolation, and troubled relationships. Untreated, PTSD doesn't go away. A wonderful website I found both useful and user friendly is: www.ncptsd.va.gov/.

Critical Incident Stress Management, conducted soon (within hours) of a traumatic event, is beneficial in preventing or minimizing PTSD. While CISM is conducted by mental health specialists (and chaplains), it is not mental therapy. It is an intervention process either one-on-one or in a group setting (no more than ten to fifteen) where people involved in the traumatic event, or witnessing the event, can discuss what they witnessed, how they feel, and how it has affected them.

Schools found that procedures designed for children, and counselors trained in these procedures, have been effective in minimizing trauma in school children.

Traumatic events involving deaths, sexual assault, trauma to a child, elements of terror in a criminal activity and incidents such as these call for a CISM debriefing.

CISM responders respond as a team where more than one person needs debriefing. The sooner people go through debriefing the better.

If several days pass between the traumatic event and the debriefing, then counseling or therapy may be needed to prevent PTSD.

APPLICABLE SCRIPTURE

I have told you these things, so that in me you may have peace. In this world you will have trouble. But take heart! I have overcome the world.

—John 16:33

Rejoice in the Lord always. I say it again: Rejoice! Let your gentleness be evident to all. The Lord is near. Do not be anxious about anything, but in everything by prayer and petition, with thanksgiving, present your requests to God. And the peace of God, which transcends all understanding, will guard your hearts and your minds in Christ Jesus."

—Philippians 4:4–7

WHAT TO PRAY FOR

- Pray for those directly involved in the event.
- Pray for the emergency responders.

- Pray for the CISM team members.

- Pray for long-term sufferers of PTSD.

- Pray for those close to PTSD sufferers.

HOW TO HELP

In my first scenario, a young woman was sexually assaulted and never received any counseling. The event occurred eleven years before she came to me, and affected her mentally and emotionally all that time. Being in a prison setting, with (aggressive but professional) male staff members, caused her anxiety leading to panic attacks. Due to the extremely long period of time since the event occurred, she needed therapy, and that was better done one-on-one, with a woman. After listening to her the day she came to me I arranged for a female psychologist in our prison to meet with her.

The second scenario was much different. Multiple people were involved, which called for a team. The traumatic event was recent. We were able to gather all but one person involved. The office was able to function smoothly in very short order.

Estimates are that eight to ten percent of the population suffers from PTSD, some are: combat veterans, firefighters, police officers, victims of sexual assault, accident victims, crime victims, and others.

There is a great chance that you know, or will know, someone with PTSD.

Your position, in ministry of someone who has been involved in, or witnessed, a traumatic event is to get professional help. The sooner a person receives help the less time they will suffer. If you become involved immediately after the traumatic event, call your county mental health agency and ask for them to send a CISM team. They will need information about the nature of the event, the location, the number of people involved, and a person to contact. Often a fire department or police chaplain may respond and they will possibly have information on how to contact a CISM team.

As a friend or family member of someone with PTSD, first recognize that they are not "crazy" as they often think they are. Either they are a victim of a crime, or a witness to a traumatic event. Generally they, or someone else, have told you what the event is.

Your function in this is to get help for your friend or family member. And to pray for them – they find comfort in that.

If the person is a veteran, the Veterans Administration hospitals and clinics have clinicians well trained and experienced in treating personnel with PTSD, these include: psychologists, psychiatrists, chaplains, counselors, and social workers.

If your friend or family member is on active duty, have them contact their base hospital or their unit chaplain. Active duty personnel often have a fear that they will be booted out on a psyche discharge. This rarely happens, but if it does they will continue to receive treatment at VA hospitals.

If your family member or friend is neither a veteran nor active duty, following are several recommendations:

1. Ask the person's primary care physician for a referral for treatment.
2. Ask your pastor (or their pastor) for a referral for a Christian counselor experienced in treating PTSD.
3. Contact your county mental health center for recommendations.
4. If your friend or family member has insurance or a HMO, contact the insurance company for referral.

People with PTSD are not crazy, they are not a danger to others, and they can't help the way they feel or act. They need treatment. They don't "just snap out of it" when told to. They often don't understand why things are happening to them. They do need your help, your understanding and support.

Family Issues

Chapter 8
Adultery

Jim is a big man, much bigger than my 5'11" frame. He called me late one night and said he needed to talk immediately. I threw on some clothes and met him downstairs in the church sanctuary. When we met Jim's pacing in front of the church told me how wound up he was.

"Pastor, you know my best friend, Gary. Well, he just told me he is messing around on his wife, Linda." Jim had been a wild man himself until nearly two years ago. He had given his heart to the Lord in a life-changing way.

"I can see this is really troubling you, Jim." I let a moment of silence hang between us before continuing. "What did you say to Gary?"

"I told him he was breaking one of the Ten Commandments; that he was sinning." Jim stood up and walked up to the church's front window. "I ought to go back down the street where I saw him and pound him into the ground!"

Although he had dedicated his life to God, he was still a little rough around the edges. Jim was such a big man; I wondered what a blow from his fist would do to his friend.

"Do you really think you should do that, Jim?"

"No, of course not, but, Pastor, what can I do?" He threw his hands up in frustration. He didn't know what to tell his friend to make him see the wrongness of his behavior, but he wanted to help him.

UNDERSTANDING THE CRISIS

While it almost seems unnecessary to define adultery, questions of "what if the couple is legally separated?" or "what if the wife/husband isn't meeting his/her physical needs" can cloud the issue. And, I will emphatically state that an open marriage is open to Satan.

Plain and simple: adultery is sin!

Adultery is one member of the marriage partnership engaging in sex with someone other than his or her spouse. Any "form" of sex in most minds is adultery, and I believe that is scriptural.

Adultery causes a tremendous amount of pain to spouses and children, and damage to relationships in extended families. It also causes serious problems in friendships, working relationships, and in churches. In every case of adultery I have dealt with, the offending party tells me that if they had known how much suffering and damage they would cause, they would have turned and run away. Not one person would say they gained a thing.

APPLICABLE SCRIPTURE

"You shall not commit adultery" Exodus 20:14.

Even before the Ten Commandments were given to the children of Israel, Abraham and his descendants recognized adultery as wrong. While traveling through Egypt, Abraham deceived Pharaoh into believing Sarah was his sister, but Pharaoh took Sarah into his harem. A plague overcame Pharaoh's household because of this act. When Isaac journeyed through the land of the Philistines, King Abimelech became angry with Isaac for stating that Rebekah was his sister. Abimelech questioned Isaac, "What is this you have done to us? One of the men might well have slept with your wife, and you would have brought guilt among us" (Genesis 26:10).

There are some great passages in Proverbs relating to adultery. Some of the best are: Proverbs 2:16–19; 6:20–29; 7:1–27.

Adultery was considered a sin in the New Testament as well. Hebrews 13:4 states that the marriage bed should be kept pure and that God will judge the adulterers and other sexually impure people.

Jesus was clear on how he viewed adultery. In Matthew 5:27–28, he states that any man who looks at a woman in lust has committed adultery in his heart. Jesus also recognized that an adulterer could change his/her life. When a woman caught in the act of adultery was brought to him, he instructed her to go and leave her life of sin (John 8:1–11).

WHAT TO PRAY FOR

- If people are Christians, pray for their restoration to God.
- Pray for the families of the adulterer.
- Pray to be granted the right words to say to the parties involved.
- Pray that no STD's (sexually transmitted diseases) or pregnancies occur.

HOW TO HELP

The initial procedures to follow depend upon if the offending party (parties) is/are Christians. If the people are Christians, I *strongly* recommend following the procedure Jesus taught in Matthew 18:15–17.

> If your brother sins against you, go and show him his fault, just between the two if you. If he listens to you, you have won your brother over. But if he will not listen, take one or two others along, "so that the matter

may be established by two or three witnesses." If he refuses to listen to them, tell it to the church; and if he refuses to listen even to the church, treat him as you would a pagan or a tax collector.

The question arises if the innocent spouse be told of the offending party's actions? This is a very touchy situation; it becomes even more so if there are children in the marriage. In my position as a Navy Chaplain, I couldn't breach confidentiality and therefore cannot speak to the spouse. However, when people ask me what to do, I counsel them to remember that the innocent spouse is now open to life-threatening STD's. The innocent spouse also needs to be protected from the family/career/financial fallout that will likely occur. I recommend that the offending spouse be given the option of telling the innocent spouse, or having someone else tell him/her.

I know this is highly controversial, but to allow sin to override the health and safety of an innocent person is, to me, irresponsible. You do risk losing a friend, but that friend was, in effect, asking you to be party to their sin and deceit by expecting you to remain silent about it.

If the offending person is not a Christian, it would not be necessary to take others from the church to them. I would, and have, separated myself from adulterers for the sake of not appearing to give approval to their deeds.

Another issue may arise if the offending party repents and asks for forgiveness. While most people rejoice at this happening, it doesn't always mean automatic forgiveness and a willingness to reconcile on the part of the offended spouse. Adultery causes deep hurt and much anguish. The offending spouse and the people around the couple must realize that it will take time, often a long time, to overcome the pain and mistrust inflicted. I *highly* encourage family counseling by a recognized Christian counselor or therapist if they choose not to use a chaplain.

You, as the pastor, lay leader, friend, or family member, have the role of giving encouragement to both parties. Consider how much faith and courage it took to repent and ask for forgiveness, and how much faith and courage it took to grant that forgiveness.

Chapter 9
Child Sexual Abuse

I met Nannette several months ago. When we recently encountered each other, the reason for her divorce was discussed. "I found out my ex-husband was sexually abusing our children."

"That must have devastated you when you found out." I was in shock myself.

Nannette nodded her head slowly. "That was over ten years ago, and my children still suffer the effects of it." I was about to ask Nannette whatever happened to her ex-husband when she continued, "He threatened to cut me into little pieces if my kids ever told me what he was doing to them." I stopped, turned, and looked at her. "It became known when my son told an emergency room nurse."

I have Nannette's permission to use her story, but due to possible legal proceedings, I will end here. My emphasis here, though, is to point out that Nanette did the right thing—she immediately took her children to a medical facility.

UNDERSTANDING THE CRISIS

Child sexual abuse is when an adult uses a minor (under the legal age of consent) for sexual gratification or exploitation. While the crimes of intercourse, rape, sodomy, and fondling are automatically assumed, in all states child sexual abuse also includes photographing a nude child, or the genitalia of a child, prostituting a child, and sexual relations of a child within marriage. Also included would be incest with a minor, pedophilia, and voyeurism where a child is viewed.

Child sexual abuse seems to be on the increase—though it could be the press coverage it is receiving. It is not a situation that is often brought into public light due to the expressed desire to protect the child victim(s).

One extremely sad truth regarding this hideous crime is that their victims often know the perpetrators. Perpetrators often are people the victims and their parents or guardians should be able to trust. Perpetrators are parents, stepparents, grandparents, aunts or uncles, cousins, parent's friend, neighbors, teachers, ministers, coaches, youth leaders, or others in positions of responsibility. Sadly, in some cases, one parent (usually the mother) knows sexual abuse is being perpetrated on her child and feels powerless to act upon it. Not acting upon it is not only immoral; it is illegal, and sinful.

The Internet compounds the issue of child sexual abuse in today's world. People who prey upon children are able to do it from the comfort and safety of their home. They pass pictures and videos of children engaging in sexual activity via e-mail and Web sites. These activities are not protected by the First Amendment, yet Constitutional restraints make it difficult to track these illegal acts.

Children logging into chat rooms and onto Web sites have fallen victim to predators. Many children have been enticed to meet strangers through seemingly innocent interactions only to find themselves victims of child sex abusers. By law, children under the age of thirteen are not allowed to log on to chat rooms, but this is nearly impossible for Internet companies to monitor.

There is no known effective treatment for child sexual abusers. Several are in trial stages, but there are no guarantees that they will be effective.

APPLICABLE SCRIPTURE

> "No one is to approach any close relative to have sexual relations. I am the LORD. Do not have sexual relations with your sister, either your father's daughter or your mother's daughter, whether she was born in the same home or elsewhere.
>
> Do not have sexual relations with your son's daughter or your daughter's daughter; that would dishonor you.

Do not have sexual relations with both a woman and her daughter. Do not have sexual relations with either her son's daughter or her daughter's daughter; they are her close relatives. That is wickedness.

Do not lie with a man as one lies with a woman; that is detestable."

—Leviticus 18:6, 9–10, 17, 22

WHAT TO PRAY FOR

- Pray for the salvation of the abuser.
- Pray for the spiritual and mental well-being of the child(ren).
- Pray for the counselor(s) treating the family.

HOW TO HELP

Truthfully, I have limited experience in working with parents of sexually abused children. Most of my experience is from having worked at a women's prison, and working with women sailors and Marines. What I find most shocking is that in what I estimate to be over half the cases, the inmates and the women sailors and Marines felt their mothers let them down, by either not believing them when they told their mothers that they were being sexually abused, or the mothers, generally

94

feeling trapped in the marriage or live-in relationship, did nothing. How sad this is. These women should have been able to trust their mothers to support and protect them. By not reporting the situation, the behavior continued.

Most states require *everyone,* with the exception of professional ministers, to report any form of child abuse, including child sexual abuse. Withholding a report due to any fear, including for personal welfare or safety, is not a legal right. Therefore, if you become aware of, or have suspicions of child abuse of any sort, you *must* report it.

The question arises, "What if the child may not be telling the truth?" You should assume the child is telling the truth for several reasons:

1. Children are not inclined to lie about sexual abuse.
2. They feel violated and shamed.
3. The child has to be protected.
4. Delaying their protection places them in jeopardy.

Sexually abused children must be taken to competent medical authorities. Due to the nature of the acts committed against them, they need to be screened for injuries—which you as a minister, parent, guardian, friend, teacher, etc., may not be able to see. The child may have internal tissue damage, which could become infected.

The sexually abused child needs to be taken to counseling immediately. The more counseling is delayed, the more guilt, fear, depression, and probably anger will set in. There is a high rate of suicide attempts among victims of child sexual abuse. The counseling will be extensive, lengthy, and require family involvement.

A common misconception I would like to alleviate here is that a child who has been sexually abused is forever emotionally scarred. The truth is that through the loving support of those around them, and competent counseling or therapy, these children can and do grow up to lead normal lives. The memories of the sexual abuse will be strong in the beginning, but over time the memories, and their damage, weakens.

Where child sexual abuse becomes a matter apart from all other forms of abuse is the nature of the perpetrator to offend again. Therefore, it is imperative to keep children away from the offender. Even post-incarceration, until the offender has proven he/she is in control of their behavior, they should not be left alone with children.

If you are a parent, or someone who monitors the computer activity of minors, closely watch what they surf on the Internet. If you find any evidence that leads you to believe they may be being stalked on the Internet *don't erase it or the site Web address.* Contact your local police department. Many predators have been caught, and children saved, as a result of caring adults notifying authorities.

In addition to the computer, recently several cases of girls being photographed in school locker rooms have been in the news. Small video cameras, easy to hide, have led to several arrests. Often these videos and pictures are passed around, or end up on the Internet. The resulting convictions have been slow, and the sentences have been short. Parents, teachers, and others need to vigorously campaign for tougher sentences where this type of invasion of privacy is concerned.

We all have the responsibility of looking out for the safety of innocent children. Whether we are parents or other relatives, teachers, neighbors, church workers, or a concerned citizen, we must stand in protection of those who cannot protect themselves.

Chapter 10
Divorce

Holding her friend by the hand, Angela entered my office. "Chaplain, Becky's husband just told her he wants a divorce. He said he's tired of being married."

I turned my chair to face both of them. "Becky, I'm sorry to hear this is happening to yo,." I said pushing a box of tissue toward her. I sat quietly waiting for her response.

"We've been married twelve years and have three kids. What am I going to do?" Wiping tears from her eyes she added, "I've stayed home with kids so I don't have any income of my own."

"Would he agree to counseling?" I questioned.

"He said he wouldn't. He already packed some of his stuff and moved in with a guy he works with." She calmed a bit as she was talking.

"I'm more than happy to counsel with you, but there are some things I also want to suggest you do." I began making a list of things for her to do. "You need to make sure you have enough money for you and the kids to get by on." The military has it way over civilians in this aspect. Commanding officers can order their personnel to provide for their dependants. "You also need to hire an attorney to protect yourself."

"But I don't want to make him mad." She appeared quite surprised by my suggestion. "And he doesn't really know what he's doing. He may want to come back home soon."

"Becky, I understand what you're saying, but you need to think of the kids and you first. It sounds to me like he's taking care of himself." Angela was nodding in agreement with me. "If he deploys without an allotment or court-ordered payment in place you could be left high and dry."

"What should I do? I don't know where to go."

"Start at the base legal office. They have information for you." I continued writing on my notepad. "But you will eventually need to hire an attorney if your husband goes through with this."

Addressing Angela I then stated, "Your job as her friend is to listen to her, but to also keep her realistic. Her kids' needs come first here. They need food, clothing, and a place to stay."

"I agree," she stated. "I'll help her through this."

I made an appointment for that afternoon for Becky to return for counseling.

UNDERSTANDING THE CRISIS

Divorce, plain and simple, is the termination of a marriage by legal means. Usually this is done by a court order.

In my experience when counseling couples, the vast majority of divorces involve one willing party, and one unwilling party. Seldom do I see it where both parties desire the divorce. This is especially true where children are involved.

Divorce is emotionally draining, heart wrenching, and generally causes families and friends to unwillingly take sides in a nasty battle. The family often includes the children.

The cost of divorce in financial terms can be devastating. In our local area (western Washington State) a couple with children and an average amount of property can expect to pay attorney fees of $15,000–$25,000 *each*! There are also filing fees, court fees, and one party is probably going to need an apartment or house to stay in.

Divorce often leads families into bankruptcy. Interestingly, when I am counseling a man who is thinking of divorce, he says he is contemplating the move due to feeling "trapped." When we examine what the financial consequences are, he often has a wake up call, and is willing to consider remaining with his family. Frequently, they are open to counseling.

The cost to the Church is tremendous. Presently, there are several high profile pastors and television-evangelists that have recently gone through divorce, or are in the process of divorce. Recent statistics I've seen indicate the divorce rate in the Church is running at the same level as in the secular world.

APPLICABLE SCRIPTURE

Has not the LORD made them one? In the flesh and spirit they are his. And why one? Because he was seeking godly offspring. So guard yourself in your spirit, and do not break faith with the wife of your youth. "I hate divorce," says the LORD.

—Malachi 2:15–16a

Some Pharisees came to him to test him. They asked, "Is it lawful for a man to divorce his wife for any and every reason?"

"Haven't you read," he replied, "that in the beginning the Creator 'made them male and female,' and said, 'For this reason a man will leave his father and mother and be united with his wife, and the two will become one flesh.' So they are no longer two but one. Therefore what God has joined together, let man not separate."

"Why then," they asked, "did Moses command that a man give his wife a certificate of divorce and send her away?" Jesus replied, "Moses permitted you to divorce your wives because your hearts were hard. But it was not this way from the beginning. I tell you that anyone who divorces his wife, except for marital unfaithfulness, and marries another woman commits adultery."

—Matthew 19:3–9

To the married I give this command (not I, but the Lord): A wife must not separate from her husband. But if she does, she must remain unmarried or else be reconciled to her husband. And a husband must not divorce his wife.

—1 Corinthians 7:10–11

Interestingly, when we look at the above passage we see that Jesus addresses one of the primary causes of divorce in the ancient days, which is the same as today, and that is hard hearts. That is what most marriage counselors, pastors, therapists, chaplains and others I have spoken with say they are dealing with in marriage counseling—hard hearts. Other words I could use are: selfishness, unforgiveness, anger, jealousy, immaturity, unloving, and sinful.

Can this be turned around?

Certainly. Scriptually speaking, I take a couple contemplating divorce through 1Corinthians 13 and Ephesians 5:22–33. I also use Galatians 5:16–26, for this passage contains living by the Spirit as opposed to living in the flesh. These three passages are more than enough to give a couple in strife a focus off of their dissention. They may focus on changing themselves, rather than focusing on what they don't like in their mate. I will allude to this more in Proceedures.

WHAT TO PRAY FOR

1. Pray for hearts to be softened.
2. Pray for both mates to be open to God.
3. Pray for both mates to open their eyes to Scriptual instruction.
4. Pray for the children involved (if any).
5. If adultery is involved, pray the "third party" will be convicted and repent.
6. Pray for the Holy Spirit to guide you as you minister to the individual/couple.
7. Pray for the marriage to be totally restored.

HOW TO HELP

I am going to divide this section into two sections. One will cover when you are able to work only with the one of the couple, the one not desiring the divorce. The second section covers if you are able to reach the couple.

If you are working with one person, as Angela was, be aware of the propensity of friends to often abandon a divorcing couple. You may be the only friend standing by as other friends try to sort out the cause and effects of divorce. This is, unfortunately, human nature as people are caught in uncertainty as to what to say, or how to respond. At this point in time, your friend is probably shaken and depressed. She needs reassurance in her value as a person, wife, and if applicable, a mother.

You may be called upon to guide your friend to counseling, or even to provide counseling to her yourself, if he/she is apprehensive about going to a professional. Only give what you are equipped to give (after prayer).

You may locate a divorce recovery program at a local church in your area. There are some excellent programs which promote healing and develop skills in areas such as single parenting, finances, and returning to dating. One program I am familiar with is called DIVORCE CARE. They offer programs through local churches by trained leaders. Their toll-free number is 1-800-489-7778. They have an excellent Web site (www.divorcecare.com), and you will be able to find the group closest to you by entering your zip code.

If your friend is being divorced by his/her mate due to unhealthy habits your friend has, such as alcoholism, drug addiction, debt, adultery, or others, encourage your friend to seek professional or group help. Do not say that the spouse will return if they see your friend seeking help and cleaning up. You can't speak for the other spouse. They should clean up regardless.

- Practice patient, effective listening. You are going to hear a wide range of emotions, doubts, and fears.
- Refrain from acting as a go-between for the couple.
- Refrain from taking sides. Even though it will be difficult, try to remain neutral and non-judgmental.
- Refrain from giving legal advice.
- Refrain from giving false hopes of reconciliation unless you see very positive signs from the other mate.
- Refrain from introducing your friend to available members of the opposite sex.
- Discourage your friend from jumping into the dating scene until all proceedings are over, and they have had time to heal.
- Encourage forgiveness.

- Encourage church attendance, if not at your church, then at one of their choice.

- Encourage the couple to view programs and/or read books on marriage and family. It might be good for you to sit in on their watching of videos.

- Encourage your friend to closely watch their spending, and refrain from loaning money. Most couples go into serious debt, and you may not ever be repaid.

- Refrain from taking on too much.

If you are able to work with the couple, I highly recommend you refer them to a professional or experienced counselor unless you are experienced. Counseling a divorce is an intense, time consuming and difficult endeavor, even with a reconciling couple. You are likely to hear things about your friend(s) you may not want to hear. Your pastor, priest, chaplain will most likely know of counselors or therapists if they don't do this type of counseling. Many choose to refer this type of counseling to marriage counseling experts. Experts often give personality assessment tests to help determine strengths and weaknesses in each mate.

If the couple is concerned about the cost of counseling, insurance companies often have coverage or co-payment plans. There may also be free or very low cost counseling available through the county mental health department, or a highly experienced pastor in the local area.

If there are children, babysitting will be necessary while the couple attends counseling, children need reassurance, children need to know they will be taken care of. Children often blame themselves for their parent's divorce and need counseling as well.

This may be the most difficult thing you have ever undertaken. It will certainly be one of the most rewarding if the couple is able to reconcile.

ADITIONAL INFORMATION

There are situations which, regretfully, occur in which I highly recommend a separation for the safety and well being of one of the spouses, and if applicable, the children. Child and/or spouse abuse, drug and/or alcohol abuse where another's safety is in jeopardy, and situations such as these, warrant the separation of the innocent party (parties) until such time as the offender receives treatment and proves his/her change in attitude and behavior.

Chapter 11
Domestic Violence

I am going to let Gina, a thirty-nine-year-old divorced mother of three, tell you her story.

"I dated Rob off and on for nine months. I saw signs of domestic violence in our relationship, but didn't recognize them as warning signs. He was possessive and very jealous. He was controlling, easily angered verbally abusive and insecure. When he was angry at me, he would spit on me, break my things, throw things, threaten to hurt me, and disappear for days at a time (he was cheating on me).

"Friends, family, neighbors, and coworkers as well as my sons' baseball coaches showed concern for my relationship, but I thought if Rob and I went to counseling things would improve.

"I didn't realize domestic violence was being directed at me until the night he became physically violent and hurt me. That night he sent me to the emergency room with multiple injuries.

"Since that night I have done two things to help myself: (1) I got out of the abusive relationship, and (2) I got help.

"I am receiving counseling, and I joined a domestic violence support group. I went to the local library and checked out books on domestic violence. I am staying in contact with the District Attorney's Office to track the case. The YWCA provided a victim advocate to walk me through the process.

"Any person who has violence used against them should receive medical attention. I was surprised at the injuries the medical people found on me that I couldn't see. You will also need their documentation for the prosecutor's office.

"I would like to warn other women not to fall into the same trap. A trap in which the man is possessive, controlling, insecure or jealous is dangerous. A man easily angered will be abusive, even if it involves breaking objects or spitting on you, your friend, family member, or coworker. Even if the relationship hasn't become physical, if all that's being experienced is degrading verbal behavior, break off the relationship *now*!!! Bear in mind, controlling behavior escalates, and it is abusive."

UNDERSTANDING THE CRISIS

Domestic Violence used to be called two separate things: Spousal/ wife abuse, and mental abuse. Now both are called domestic violence.

Domestic violence occurs in small town and big cities. It occurs in all races, economic strata, education levels, and religions: men abuse and women abuse; husbands and wives abuse; boyfriends, girlfriends, and fiancés abuse; gay partners' abuse. No one is exempt from the potential of having violence used against them unless they are cautious in selecting their friendships and relationships.

Following are two separate lists. The first is a list of warning signs a spouse or partner may exhibit that he/she may be an abuser. The second list contains warning signs of a victim.

Warning Signs of an Abuser:

- Checking up on their partner too much, screening phone calls, mail, where the person was and who they were with, calling several times a day

- Explosive temper

- Forcing sex, possibly including deviant sex, on their partner

- Touching in hurtful or other inappropriate ways

- Rushing the relationship, asking quickly for commitments

- Blaming partner, or others, for their shortcomings

- Destroying (or threatening) property, especially cherished mementos
- Jealousy and possessiveness
- Isolating partner from previous relationships, especially family
- Abusing pets
- Demeaning and /or humiliating partner in public and private
- Keeping partners from church, support groups, counselors
- Past history of violent behavior and/or substance abuse
- Early on makes the decisions in the relationship

Warning Signs of a Victim:

- Is unexpectedly absent from work, school, church, other activities
- Has personality changes, including low self-esteem
- Has a fear of their partner
- Inappropriate blaming of self for partner's behavior
- Signs of injuries with excuses that don't make sense
- Seems to be isolated, withdrawn
- Abusive or aggressive toward children
- Indecisiveness
- Seems to be losing possessions
- Is being "checked-on" by partner
- Being humiliated by partner

- Is being rushed in their relationship
- Changes appearance to suit partner

The primary thing for you, as a pastor, family member or friend, to remember about domestic violence is that it is an issue of *control*. If a woman (the primary victims) is living with or dating an abuser, no matter how clean she keeps her home, no matter how well behaved the children are, no matter how much money is in the bank, or how well she cooks, the abuse will continue. It is through violence, or the threat of violence, that the abuser's will is enforced upon the victim. The violence escalates as it continues because the woman feels powerless to make it stop, and she fears leaving the relationship.

I used the status of the man being the abuser and the woman being the victim, but there are many cases of men being the victims of domestic violence. Estimates vary of men being victims in twenty to forty percent of cases. Just as women are afraid or ashamed to report their situations, the same is true for men. The same is also true in gay and lesbian relationships.

Allowing abuse to continue makes the abused an enabler. This is true also for those who have knowledge of the abuse and refuse to take action (friends, family, coworkers, fellow students, neighbors, etc.). *An enabler is one who feeds the addiction of the addicted person.* In this case, *the addicted person is addicted to violence and control,* much the same way an alcoholic is addicted to alcohol. And just as an enabler would give the addicted person money to purchase alcohol, an enabler will not report violence and let it continue.

I have never known an abuser to just stop their behavior. In only one situation did I see a man change due to receiving Christ, but most abusers don't want to change. The most successful methods of bringing beneficial change has been for the police to be called into the home and courts to force change. I've seen abusers become Christians after this action is initiated. Thus, if the abuser avoids being counseled then the authorities must be called in. More about this will be discussed in How to Help.

APPLICABLE SCRIPTURE

For the abuser:

Better a patient man than a warrior, a man who controls

his temper than one who takes a city.

—Proverbs 16:32

The acts of the sinful nature are obvious…fits of rage.

—Galatians 5:19, 20

Husbands, love your wives, just as Christ loved the church and gave himself up for her to make her holy, cleansing her by the washing with water through the word, and to present her to himself as a radiant church, without stain or wrinkle or any other blemish, but holy and blameless. In this same way, husbands ought to love their own bodies. He who loves his wife loves himself. However, each one of you must love his wife as he loves himself.

—Ephesians 5:25–28, 33a

Husbands, love your wives and do not be harsh with them.

—Colossians 3:19

Love is patient, love is kind…. It is not easily angered.

—1 Corinthians 13:4a, 5b

For the abused:

Therefore, if anyone is in Christ, he is a new creation; the old has gone, the new has come.

—2 Corinthians 5:17

For you did not receive a spirit that makes you a slave again to fear, but you received the Spirit of sonship. And by him we cry, *"Abba,* Father." The Spirit himself testifies with our spirit that we are God's children. Now if we are children, then we are heirs—heirs of God and co-heirs with Christ.

—Romans 8:15–17a

Do not be yoked together with unbelievers. For what do righteousness and wickedness have in common? Or what fellowship can light have with darkness? … What does a believer have in common with an unbeliever?

—2 Corinthians 6:14, 15b

WHAT TO PRAY FOR

- Pray for the safety and healing of the abused.
- Pray for the abuser to repent of his/her ways.
- Pray for quality intervention.
- Pray for the cycle of codependency (enabling) to end.
- Pray for God to guide you on what you should say and do.
- Pray for any children involved.

HOW TO HELP

This is an extremely difficult situation to work for several reasons. First of all, the primary concern for most people is the safety of the victim. Yet, in trying to help the victim the abuser often feels threatened, he (or she) will lose control. He will generally take measures to protect his situation. In an emergency, the best suggestion is to have the courts issue a protection order. If the abuser is likely to violate the order, then emergency accommodations should be used if the abuser is not incarcerated. A plan must be in place, ready to implement, before actions are taken. The plan should include accommodations, funds, legal help, counseling, and job training (if necessary). All involved must bear safety in mind for the victim.

The victim must have counseling to elevate her own perception of herself. If through abuse she has a low perception of her self worth, she will likely drop any program and return to an abusive relationship. When I work with abuse victims I use Dr. Lawrence Crabb Jr.'s method of counseling found in his books *Basic Principles of Biblical Counseling* (Zondervan) and *Effective Biblical Counseling* (Zondervan).

It is common for the victims to have doubts about their actions. They need to be encouraged to stay the course. To stop the help would be to encourage the abuser to continue his immoral and illegal actions. This would be where you, the friend or family member, uses Crabb's approach to help the abused. If you follow Crabb closely, you have a good chance of being successful. His basic six-step approach looks something like this:

1. Identify negative feelings which are compounded by negative behavior.

2. Identify negative behavior (which, along with negative feelings, is caused by wrong thinking).

3. Identify wrong thinking.

4. Promote right thinking.

5. Plan right behavior produced by right thinking.

6. Identify satisfying feelings produced by right behavior and right thinking.

Without changing the victim's thinking, little will be accomplished. Another book, which I believe is great to go through with a victim of abuse is, *Telling Yourself the Truth* by William Backus and Marie Chapman (Bethany House). This book contains its own study guide, which a friend or counselor may go over with the victim.

The first step, then, would be to identify why the abused feels (and thinks) she needs to be in this relationship. Once the feelings and thinking are identified, then the second step begins. Through *loving and gentle* persuasion (counseling) right thinking, which leads to right behavior and feelings (Crabb steps 4–6) takes place. The counselee/

abused must internalize this process for it to be effective. In my own experience in counseling people, I have seen the process take as little as two days (rare), or as long as months. If forced to give an average, I would say approximately a month of nearly daily contact by family members.

As far as the overall abuse situation, there are multiple ways of removing the abused from the presence of the abuser. First, an evaluation must be made of the safety of the victims, as well as those providing assistance. Is the abuser likely to brandish a weapon, and if so, is he likely to use it? Should governmental authorities (police, court, and protective services) be called in prior to removing the abuser or victim from the home/relationship? Should a court issued restraining order (also called a no contact order or order of protection) be issued?

Often the process is started by a 911 telephone call, reporting domestic violence. In many states, laws mandate that if domestic violence has occurred then one party has to go to jail. In the military, the Family Advocacy program is automatically implemented, and the abuser is mandated into a treatment program.

Second, consideration must be made as to what assistance the family, church, or governmental agencies will give the victim for housing and food, and if necessary, for employment or job training. If the abused has been removed from her birth family environment, she may wish to return, and transportation may be necessary.

Not only does the immediate family have to be together on the support for a person leaving a life of abuse, but the "community" around the victim needs to be supportive as well. The church, co-workers, friends, and neighbors need to be encouraging, emotionally and mentally supportive, and honest if they see "slippage" in the recovery process.

Where I have seen difficulty is in the abuser's family trying to encourage the couple to remain together—without the abuser receiving treatment, and often asking the victim to overlook his "one bad habit." The other difficulty I have seen is when church members tell the victim that they do not have biblical grounds for separation or divorce. While biblical grounds for divorce may be lacking, separation for safety is warranted.

There are many community support agencies that provide shelters for abused women and children. Among them are St. Vincent DePaul, Salvation Army, military, and generally large towns, and counties. Try to be aware of what is available and what the requirements are in advance of intervention.

Chapter 12
Gay or Lesbian Child

I was in my office putting my jacket on to go to lunch when one of my assistants stepped in. "Chaplain, there is a lady on the phone saying she needs to talk to a chaplain. She won't say why or who she is."

This is usually not good news. I nodded my head and sat in my chair, saying a quick, silent prayer. Then I picked up the phone.

"Chaplain Scott speaking…."

"Oh Chaplain, my husband is at sea and I don't know what to do." Her voice was heavy with emotion.

"What is the situation? What's going on?" I couldn't place the voice; I had no idea who she was.

"It's my son. He's a senior in high school. My daughter just told me he's gay." She was now fully crying. "I don't know how to tell my husband."

UNDERSTANDING THE CRISIS

The issue of homosexuality has torn families, churches, clubs, schools, and other organizations apart. This topic has affected local, state, and federal elections. On one end of the theological and political spectrum the belief is that homosexuality is natural, that in some people their genetic makeup leads them to be attracted to members of their own sex. In this view, a gay or lesbian can neither be healed nor changed into a heterosexual person. Thus, in their belief, homosexuality is neither a sin nor morally wrong.

On the other end of the spectrum is the belief homosexuality is sinful, and thus is morally wrong. Their belief is gays and lesbians can repent, be forgiven, and then lead a heterosexual life.

This book is designed to help people aid parishioners, friends, and family in crisis situations. In this chapter the person needing help is the parent of a gay or lesbian. Therefore I will not be dealing with the issue of homosexuality, instead addressing helping parents cope.

Parents, particularly conservative ones, are shocked by the news. They fear for their child's salvation, safety, and image. They question their parenting skills, their image in church, extended family, and community. In my experience in working with gays, and parents of gays, the underlying feeling parents have is homosexuality is the worst of sins—even more so than murder.

This is especially so where men or boys are involved. This can be readily observed among Hollywood celebrities where women who have publicly stated their orientation are more vocal than men, and seem to be accepted by society more. I state this not to draw a distinction between gays and lesbians. My point is if you are helping the parents of a gay man, it would be best not to tell them how the family of a lesbian has coped. There is a difference.

If there are other children in the family, siblings will most likely need the same help as their parents. However, the siblings, especially if they are young, are more likely to have their feelings internalized.

A person who has been sexually assaulted by a member or members of the same sex is not homosexual. While in ministry, I have counseled many men and women who were sexually assaulted by the same gender. They were victims of sexual assault, not oriented toward homosexuality.

APPLICABLE SCRIPTURE

The emphasis here is in helping the parents cope. Therefore I am including only verses applicable to that, rather than those condemning homosexual conduct. In reality the Bible does not specifically address the issue of being the parents of a gay man or woman.

Refrain from anger and turn from wrath; do not fret—
it leads only to evil. For evil men will be cut off, but
those who hope in the LORD will inherit the land.

—Psalm 37:8–9

[Note: In the verse from Psalm 37, focus on turning
from anger and wrath and hoping in the Lord, not on
the evil men.]

So I say to you: Ask and it will be given to you; seek
and you will find; knock and the door will be opened to
you. For everyone who asks receives; he who seeks finds;
and to him who knocks, the door will be opened.

—Luke 11:9–10

Fathers, do not embitter your children, or they will
become discouraged.

—Colossians 3:21

[Note: I include the verse above to encourage parents
to keep communications with their child.]

Humble yourselves, therefore, under God's mighty
hand, that he may lift you up in due time. Cast all your
anxiety on him because he cares for you.

—1 Peter 5:6–7

WHAT TO PRAY FOR

- Pray for the gay child's relationship with God.
- Pray for the health and safety of the gay child.
- Pray for the relationship between the parents and their child.
- Pray for the marriage of the parents.
- Pray for the siblings (if any) and other extended family members.
- Pray for the faith of the parents.

HOW TO HELP

This will be very difficult for you to function in. You've probably known the child for years, maybe even decades. Your first instinct may be to confront him or her, and describe the pain they are causing their parents. Don't!! I say this for two reasons: the parents have most likely made their feelings known, and the parents need your entire focus.

The parents will probably go through a grieving process much like that of someone who is dying. In fact, they are experiencing a loss of their dreams and expectations, and even the life they anticipated for their child. I observed this in two sets of parents. I'll review the five stages of the Kubler-Ross process and explain how it would apply in this setting.

1. **Denial and isolation:** Parents literally can't believe their child is gay. They fear others will find out.
2. **Anger**: Parents are angry at their child for revealing of their sexuality. They may be angry and blame each other.
3. **Bargaining:** Parents are likely to disbelieve their child, rationalizing that the child is confused.
4. **Depression:** Parents become deeply depressed fearing for their child's salvation and health. They tend to blame themselves as parents.
5. **Acceptance:** Not always easy, especially with conservative Christians.

The more you are aware of this process the more you will be able to help them through it. The best way to help parents and siblings is to listen, and to answer their questions.

Parents may choose to cut ties with their child. While I was a prison chaplain parents tended to maintain contact with inmates convicted of drug crimes, homicide, and various other crimes—but I've seen where openly gay children have been cut off from their families.

Often these children go into depression and despair, and sometimes turn to dangerous practices, such as drugs, eating disorders, and may lead to suicidal attempts. Many of the online resources I used report a high instance of suicide and suicide attempts among the homosexual population, especially among young men.

Encourage parents and siblings to maintain their relationship with the child. Families who maintain contact seldom see these behaviors in their children.

ADDENDUM

At some point, parents will probably ask you how they can change their child. The truth is they can't change their child. From an evangelical perspective only God, by faith in Christ Jesus, can change their child. However, if they would like information on ministries to gays there is one I would recommend called Exodus International (www.exodus-international). They have an excellent Web site.

For a non-evangelical resource which discusses the differences in conservative and liberal theological views I recommend Religious Tolerance (www.religioustolerance.org/). This, too, is an excellent Web site which has links to many other resources.

Chapter 13
Rebellious Child

"I have to call Jason and make certain he hasn't taken off," Patricia said as she arrived at our door. She took her cell-phone out of her pocket as she greeted me.

"Sure, I understand," I nodded slowly. My response was automatic. We had started a home fellowship group two weeks before, and this was her first evening with us. As I walked into the living room, to give her privacy for her phone call, I reflected on her situation.

Patricia and her family lived on the same overseas base we lived on. Patricia was a loving and caring mother and had a great job as a Department of Defense civilian employee. Jason, her seventeen year old son, was rebellious. He had stolen her car three weeks earlier, and had been confined to his house by the commanding officer, except for when he had to be at school or when his mother and sister attended church.

When I spoke to Jason and asked him why he rebelled, he couldn't tell me. I believed him when he said he didn't know. I understood the reasons for rebellion vary, children can rebel against either lax parents or strict parents, and this can be confusing to both parents and children.

Patricia joined our group in the living room as she put her cell phone away. "He's one step from being put on medication, and we're one step from having to return to the U.S.," and then she began to cry.

UNDERSTANDING THE CRISIS

This chapter is written directly for the reader with a rebellious child. The method for helping a family with a rebellious child is to listen and encourage. However, too much listening may delay a family from seeking professional help—which I will discuss later.

Times are much different from when I grew up (late 1950s-early 1970s). Both my mother and my father spanked me. My maternal grandmother, who was only 4'11" tall used to make my cousin and me climb trees to cut switches for her to use on us when we misbehaved. My third grade teacher broke a yardstick across my behind when I acted squirrelly while doing math problems on the chalkboard. Now days, any of those practices could land a parent or teacher in jail. The teacher assuredly would be fired. So what is a parent to do?

My wife and I were parenting experts until we had children. We read all of Dr. Dobson's books, we knew the pertinent parenting verses of the Bible, and we had observed successful parents. We were, in fact, just like most Christian parents. Then we had kids.

The problem parents face is that most physical forms of (corporal) punishment can't be used in today's society. Whereas in biblical times parents were told to use a rod (much more than grandma's switches) to discipline children. Now parents are generally limited to issuing timeouts, restriction/grounding, and withholding privileges. As many parents have found, though, a rebellious child will often break restriction, or throw tantrums when told to go for a timeout. Attempts to punish seem to lead to more rebellion, which lead to more frustration and heartache.

During these times parents are also faced with doubt. They doubt their faith, they doubt God's support, and they doubt their church's support. I know. I've been there. There is hope. I know many wonderful Christian men and women who were rebellious children. There are some famous Christians, such as Franklin Graham, son of Billy Graham, whose testimonies include their time of rebellion against God and against their parents.

APPLICABLE SCRIPTURE

There are two sections of applicable Scriptures here. The first will have to do with sharing wisdom with your child. Even though your child is in rebellion, continue to do what the Bible says. Share God's wisdom with your child. Most of these Scriptures are from the first nine chapters of Proverbs. Below are only two examples of many applicable verses from Proverbs.

The second group of Scripture is for your assurance that God knows what you are going through.

> Listen, my son, to your father's instruction and do not forsake your mother's teaching. They will be a garland to grace your head and a chain to adorn your neck. My son, if sinners entice you, do not give in to them. My son, do not go along with them, do not set foot on their paths.
> —Proverbs 1:8–10, 15

> My son, if you accept my words and store up my commands within you, turning your ear to wisdom and applying your heart to understanding, and if you call out for insight and cry aloud for understanding, and if you look for it as for silver and search for it as for

hidden treasure, then you will understand the fear of the LORD and find the knowledge of God. For the LORD gives wisdom, and from his mouth come knowledge and understanding. He holds victory in store for the upright, he is a shield to those whose walk is blameless, for he guards the course of the just and protects the way of his faithful ones.

—Proverbs 2:1–8

Jesus replied, "I tell you the truth, if you have faith and do not doubt, not only can you do what was done to the fig tree, but also you can say to this mountain, 'Go, throw yourself into the sea,' and it will be done. If you believe, you will receive whatever you ask for in prayer."

—Matthew 21:21–22

I tell you the truth, my Father will give you whatever you ask in my name.... Ask and you will receive, and your joy will be complete.

—John 16:23

WHAT TO PRAY FOR

- Pray for the restoration of your child to God.

- Pray for the restoration of your child to your family.

- Pray for Christians to be put in your child's path.

- Pray for support from family, friends, and church.

HOW TO HELP

First, let's discuss what rebellion is not. Hyperactivity is not rebellion. Hyperactivity is generally a medical condition. Laziness and moodiness are not rebellion.

Rebellion is the willful disregard for the will and direction of the parents. This would include step-parents, adoptive parents, and guardians. The rebellion spreads to school, other homes, and often unless it is stopped, goes into breaking the law.

The first thing to do when confronted with a rebellious child is to communicate openly. Often the behavior results from frustration over a condition such as: a learning disability, a physical impediment, or something else causing a feeling of inadequacy. Through counseling the problem facing your child may be overcome.

Children experiencing parental divorce, children who have been assaulted, and children going through the separation of a parent often act out. Three reasons I have seen for this are:

1. The child believing the separation is their fault.

2. The child's world is being badly shaken and torn apart.

3. The children don't have the experience yet to deal with these circumstances.

In these situations your family needs therapy. The younger your child is, and the sooner the problem is addressed, the greater chance there is for success. In this type of family therapy there may be two therapists used—one for your child, and one for your family.

If you are facing an older child rebelling, try to make maximum use of your resources. This includes school counselors, family members, youth pastors, or any trusted person who your child may open up to. This is not the time to act out of hurt feelings because your child won't talk to you. Sometimes it's easier for them to talk to someone else. Be humble and accept help.

In the event your child refuses help, you have tough decisions to make.

Rebellious behavior usually escalates. Unchecked, the child begins to feel he or she is in control of the home and family. Outside the home they feel invincible as far as rules and laws are concerned. Patterns of narcissistic thinking often develop. This is especially so if the child is above average in intelligence or abilities.

Determine early where "the line" is, that is the point where your child will no longer be allowed in your home because of their behavior. Make this point known. Enforce it. I have seen parents call the police because they found drugs in their home. I have seen parents change locks on the doors after their child stole from them. Not responding strongly would cause you to be victims over and over again.

You, the reader, may be thinking this is harsh, and you're right, it is harsh. However, if your child knew where the line was and chose to cross it, he is responsible for his consequences. Often it is experiencing harsh consequences that cause a child (even an adult child) to begin cooperating. Removing this child from your home will also allow the rest of your family to begin healing.

Don't ever stop praying for your child. Don't ever stop loving your child. Don't ever stop caring for your child. Don't ever stop hoping for your child. There is always hope for them. I know many men and women who were rebellious when they were younger, and now they are successful in ministry, in medicine, in business, in the military, and as parents.

FOLLOW THROUGH

While this chapter was written directly to the parents of a rebellious child, I do want to address the friends and families of those parents.

Often the parents of a rebellious child are isolated by their situation. They feel like failures, even though their other children are well behaved. Their feelings of isolation and failure can lead to feelings of despair and depression, and have led to the breakup of marriages.

These families need your support. They need their friends, families, church, and neighbors to rally around them and care for them. It will be difficult for them to overcome their feelings of despair and depression. A rebellious child situation can last for several years, even well past the child's eighteenth birthday.

Be willing to listen to the parents vent their frustrations. Encourage them to be involved in church. Spend time with them. At times you may see where a parent, or both parents, needs to make a behavioral change. I recommend you make the suggestion in a gentle nudging way. You may need to suggest the family seek counseling with a pastor or therapist. If the family isn't connected with a church your pastor could recommend an excellent counselor or therapist.

Death

Chapter 14
Death of a Child

I pulled into the parking lot outside the headquarters office building when my assistant rushed out. "The hospital emergency room called, they're looking for you." I had volunteered to cover for the Naval Hospital Protestant chaplain while he was on leave. My family attended the service at the chapel next to the hospital.

"Did they say why?" I asked as I put my old Mazda van in reverse.

"Yes, a baby died just a little while ago. The parents want a chaplain to be with them." I nodded and drove out of the parking lot, praying for the parents, as well as for myself. My wife and I have four children, and I couldn't imagine going through what the parents were experiencing.

When I entered the emergency room, a Marine corporal was waiting for me. "Sir, you'll find Sgt. Wilson and his wife waiting for you in the prayer chapel. I'll escort you." I knew where the prayer chapel was, but this Marine wanted to be helpful, and I could ask him questions as we walked. It would be far better than asking the parents.

"Thank you. Do you know how old the baby was?" I questioned.

"I believe he was less than a week old."

"Do they have other children?" I asked, thinking ahead to flying them back to the United States, we had to ensure enough seats on the plane.

"No, Sir, this was their first child."

I asked more relevant questions until we reached the prayer chapel. I was going to ask the young marine to wait outside when he stated, "I'll stand by the door and keep others from coming in, except those who need to come in, Sir."

I gave him my thanks and entered the chapel.

Tom and Sherrie were sitting holding hands. I moved a chair around to face them and sat down. A small trash can next to Sherrie was nearly full of tissue. Without my having said a word, Tom said, "Thanks for coming, Chaplain." Sherrie nodded in agreement.

"You are welcome. And, I am so very sorry for the loss of your son."

Both parents looked tired and numb. They were in shock.

EXPLANATION

There is no circumstance quite as shocking or taxing as the event of a child's death. In nearly everyone's view, children, especially infants, are not supposed to die. Even when a child is an adult, in the parents' and grandparents' view, the child is supposed to outlive them.

Therefore, it is important to understand that you should not treat this event as you would if an adult died. It is not a routine funeral planning situation. Rather, much more than anything else, it is ministering to parents, grandparents, other family, and close friends. A ministry to the seriously suffering, resulting from the loss of a child, requires a lot of silence, patience, listening, comforting, praying with the family, and grieving on your own part. If you aren't grieving with them, it might be best if you aren't with them.

The vast majority of child deaths are caused by accidents and violence rather than illness. As a result, people in the surrounding community, family, close friends and associates (teachers, neighbors) in particular, need someone or something at which to vent their anger, frustration, and often hostility.

When circumstances such as the death, or even the serious injury or illness of a child occur, people feel powerless. All of their efforts at parenting, protecting their child, all of their love and devotion, seem to be for naught as they consider their child's situation. And generally, in the event of illness or serious accident, there seems to be nothing they can do. When death occurs, they often focus their anger and frustration at God.

You, as a close friend or family member, may feel powerless as well. This is generally not an effective time to defend God; most parents are not in a frame of mind to listen. The parents will be in a better position to listen in a few days, or a week or two. After the parents calm down they will often apologize for things they said about God if they were offensive. Listen, and accept their apology.

The death or serious injury to a child often leads to the breakup of the parents. They often become involved in the "blame game," blaming each other for the event. Where a serious illness strikes a child, one parent will often leave because they can not handle the pressure, or do not want to be present.

APPLICABLE SCRIPTURE

Precious in the sight of the LORD is the death of his saints.

—Psalm 116:15

People were also bringing babies to Jesus to have him touch them. When the disciples saw this, they rebuked them. But Jesus called the children to him and said,

"Let the little children come to me, and do not hinder them, for the Kingdom of God belongs to such as these."

—Luke 18:15–16

WHAT TO PRAY FOR

- Pray for the parents.
- Pray for all other family members.
- Pray for the community.
- Pray for anyone involved in counseling the family.

HOW TO HELP

One of the first things to remember when approaching the family is to say something like, "I'm sorry for your loss, and I want to help in any way I can." *Do not* in any way give any of the old platitudes, the clichés of, "your child isn't suffering anymore," or "you can always have another child." These statements actually cause the family more grief and pain.

In this situation, you will probably hear things from family, friends, neighbors, or others that offend you. God may be blamed for causing the death, illness, or injury, or he may be blamed for not preventing it.

Listen, be compassionate; you don't need to defend God. This is simply anger and frustration speaking out. Your faith isn't being tested, and any defense you make could escalate the situation.

If you become involved in the situation soon after it occurs, notify the family's pastor if they have one. The pastor should become immediately involved as well. If the family does not attend church, bring your own pastor into the situation, *if* the family gives permission. Your pastor will be able to provide grief counseling, as well as help set up the funeral arrangements. If this is a young family with little or no savings, your pastor will likely know of funds to help defray medical and funeral expenses.

If it was an accidental death or tragic circumstance, the people who witnessed the event should be taken through a Critical Incident Stress Debrief. Generally if the event happened on or near school grounds, students, teachers, and staff will undergo this highly beneficial service. Often the responding emergency workers will as well. However, witnesses, children not near schools, and family, seldom do. Emergency workers, county mental health, chaplains, hospital counselors, and often pastors know who to contact to put a Critical Incident Debrief in place. There is a significant impact in recovery for those who go through a CISD and those who do not.

When helping a family who has suffered the death, injury, or serious illness of a child, you need to be prepared for long-term involvement.

Certain dates, such as the birthdays of the child, the anniversary of the child's death, will have a major impact on the family for many years. It is appropriate to send cards, flowers, a food basket, or other token on these occasions. You won't be bringing up old or painful memories. The family will already be remembering on these days. They will appreciate your show of love and support.

As soon as they are able, the family should go into grief counseling. This counseling will help the family work through their grief, open up communications with each other, and help prevent the "blame game." Due to frustration, powerlessness, anger, and despair, parents often say things to each other which they otherwise wouldn't say. Grief counselors watch for this and help couples work through it.

Generally families who have undergone a tragic circumstance ask a close family member or friend to be their spokesperson. If you become that person, remember, the media loves a feeding frenzy. I strongly recommend you be brief, succinct, factual as possible, and boldly ask for privacy. The media, in the event the death or injury resulted from an accident or tragic circumstance, may try to have you lay blame or personally indict the person thought to be responsible. I highly recommend against doing this. I have seen where this has come back to haunt the spokesperson, and it only adds to the pain and suffering.

Be prepared for calls from lawyers. I urge you to take messages, and do not to put the family on the phone. Let the family grieve in peace if they so wish. If someone was at fault for the child's death or injuries, there will be plenty of time to sue if they wish to do so.

There are support groups for families who have undergone this type of tragedy. They are mainly found in larger towns and cities. Check with your pastor, the county metal health agency, or hospital mental health department for one close to you. A counselor or social worker may also be aware of other families in your area who have suffered similar circumstances. They may refer you to a support group such as *The Compassionate Friends*. This wonderful, non-profit organization uses seasoned grievers to reach out to families recently suffering the death of a child. There are no memberships, due, or fees involved. Their only mission is to help families through the grief process. Their toll-free number is 1-877-969-0010. They also have a Web site (www.compassionatefriends.org/).

I recommend providing help such as mowing the lawn, cooking, driving, taking phone calls, and other things to help the family during their serious time of grief and shock. If there is a reception after the funeral, offer to set it up and clean up afterwards.

It may take a long time, but unless there is another child, eventually the parents will put away or dispose of items belonging to the child—toys, clothing, car seats, etc. This will be highly emotional or even traumatic for them, and they may need your spiritual and emotional support.

FOLLOW UP

Tom and Sherrie's unit chaplain was back in the United States on leave, but their Major Command chaplain arrived about an hour after I did. He helped the unit arrange for the family to return to the U.S. for the funeral and burial of their baby. Upon their return to Okinawa, the unit chaplain arranged for grief counseling for Tom and Sherrie.

Chapter 15
Death of a Loved One

Entering my office with a young Marine in tow, the Admin Officer stated, "Chaplain, the Lance Corporal here was just advised his brother died in a car wreck early this morning."

Rising from my chair I took the Marine's hand and gave him a firm handshake. I motioned them to a couch in my office and closed the door. "I am very sorry to hear about your brother's death," I said.

"Thank you, Chaplain," Lance Corporal Ramirez replied. I could see he was fighting hard not to break into tears.

"When is the funeral," I asked.

"I'm supposed to call in a while and find out," the Marine replied in a soft voice.

"Sir," the Admin Officer caught my attention. "The Lance Corporal has never been to a funeral, and frankly, I have attended only military ones. He would like to know what he should do."

I nodded my head, but focused my attention back on the young Marine who suffered the loss. "I understand you need to know what to do about the funeral. But more importantly, Lance Corporal Ramirez, I want you to know that it's OK for you to feel emotions regarding the loss of your brother. You look like you're about to burst right now. Have you cried yet?"

"No, Sir, I'm a marine," he replied.

I was about to respond when there was a knock at my door and the Sergeant Major entered my office.

"Sorry to intrude, Chaplain, but I heard about Lance Corporal Ramirez and I was told he was here."

Sergeant Major Garcia is a Marine's Marine. He wore more ribbons on his uniform than any man I knew. The creases on his camouflage uniforms were razor sharp and could probably draw blood. He quickly moved next to Lance Corporal Ramirez, took his arms, stood him up, and embraced the young, hurting Marine in a bear hug.

"Hey man, I am so sorry to hear about your brother." Sgt. Maj. Garcia rocked the fellow Marine from side to side for about twenty seconds, and then they sat on the couch.

I knew Sgt. Maj. Garcia to be a polished professional, yet also knew him to be a feeling human being, not afraid of emotions. "Sergeant Major, I was just telling Lance Corporal Ramirez that it's alright to feel the emotions of his loss."

"You got that right, Chaplain," Sgt. Maj. Garcia stated. He knew exactly where I was going, what I was saying. "I was a Staff Sergeant when my father passed away. I cried at the funeral even though I was in my dress uniform." He looked Ramirez in the eyes, "Real men, real Marines, cry."

At that the junior Marine let the tears flow, and the Sergeant major and Admin Officer both put their arms around their brother Marine.

Later that day, a good friend drove Lance Corporal Ramirez to the airport and saw him onto the plane. His work section took a collection and sent a beautiful bouquet to the funeral.

UNDERSTANDING THE CRISIS

The death of a loved one can strike at a young age, or may not affect someone until they are in their thirties (which is the latest I have seen it). It may be expected as in the case of a loved one who has suffered a long serious illness, or it may be totally unexpected as in the situation with the Marine, Lance Corporal Ramirez. Regardless of how the death occurred, my focus here will be on what you, as friend, should focus on. In short, the manner of the decedent's death isn't as relevant as what you do as a caring friend.

Upon hearing of the death of a loved one (could be family, friend, or in some cases could be someone famous they've never met, people will experience a wide range of emotions, as happened at the deaths of President Kennedy, Elvis Presley, and Princess Diana), people will generally go through just as if they knew the person. The most common emotions tend to be, but are not limited to, shock, doubt/disbelief, sorrow, anger, grief, loss, confusion, and others. Often they may experience more than one emotion at a time.

People express emotions differently. Some will express vocally with crying, yelling, moaning, and lots of talking. Others may sit quietly and emote. You may not necessarily be comfortable with their method, but as long as they appear safe and healthy, allow them to process as they choose.

APPLICABLE SCRIPTURE

There are many biblical passages having to do with death. However, what you have to consider before whipping your Bible out and quoting Scripture is that people who aren't Christians may be confused when you speak of the Resurrection or eternal judgment. At this point in their grief they need to hear passages of comfort and peace, of God's love and mercy.

During times of grief people appreciate familiar scriptural passages. Even non-churchgoing people tend to appreciate hearing Psalms 23. This gives them comfort and often brings back pleasant memories.

One other passage which is often familiar to non-church goers/non-Christians is Ecclesiastes 3:1–8, although I generally include verses 9–13. It was used in a hit song in the 1960s. Here is a partial quote of the passage:

> There is a time for everything, and a season for every
> activity under heaven:
> A time to be born and a time to die, a time to plant and
> a time to uproot ... a time to weep and a time to laugh,
> a time to mourn and a time to dance.

If the people you are working with are Christians, and the deceased was a believer, there are several excellent Bible passages. 1 Corinthians 15 speaks of the resurrection and I have found this to be quite comforting to Christians. John 14:1–4, especially verse 2 where Jesus states he is going to prepare a place for us is an excellent and well received passage. One other passage I recommend is Job 19:25–27. In this passage Job states that even after his flesh is destroyed he will see God.

WHAT TO PRAY FOR

- Pray for God to grant you wisdom and guidance.

- Pray for God to give peace and comfort to your friend's family.

- Pray for all funeral and memorial arrangements to go smoothly.

HOW TO HELP

Try not to push them through their emotions, just allow them to feel what they are feeling. The most important thing for you to do at this time is to listen, and if they ask you questions, answer honestly.

It is not appropriate for you to tell the friends or family that the deceased is in a better place. There are two reasons for this. The first is the family may be grieving their loss, and their future loneliness rather than the location of the deceased. Secondly, if you didn't know the deceased, and if he/she wasn't a Christian, you may cause the family/ friends to doubt your sincerity. However, if the family/friends state that the deceased is in a better place, is suffering no pain, or words such as those, it is highly appropriate for you to agree (if applicable).

If you are able to help the family/friends make funeral arrangements, travel plans, meals, phone calls, or helps such as those, your efforts will be appreciated. Driving is often a major chore for family/

friends as they tend to be distracted by events. A simple chore, such as driving an obituary to the newspaper, is generally appreciated.

Helping such as cooking, cleaning, preparing the home for guests, mowing the lawn and other yard maintenance, things the family doesn't have the time or energy for is generally appreciated.

Most funeral homes are honest and professional businesses. However, there are others which are an embarrassment to the funeral industry through their efforts to gouge money out of the bereaved. Be alert to the costs quoted to the family/friends if you are with them when arrangements are made. If you think something doesn't sound right, try and mention it in a sensitive and timely manner.

Many families are electing cremation for their deceased loved ones. According to a recent survey I read, this is happening in approximately one-quarter of all funeral arrangements. If this is something you are against for one reason or another, this in not the time to voice your beliefs or opinion on the matter. This is the family's decision to make.

If a negligent or wrongful death occurred, attorneys may overwhelm the family with phone calls. You may be called upon to screen calls. Be firm, be polite, and take messages. If the family elects to sue they have considerable time, often years to file a lawsuit. You may encourage them to choose a reputable lawyer in your local area, rather than to pick the splashiest TV or yellow pages advertisement. Consulting several attorneys is a good idea.

If the media becomes involved, support their decision to speak to the press or to remain silent, whichever they choose to do.

The affects of the death of a loved one may mean considerable changes for some family members. It could mean a move to a nursing home for a surviving spouse, the sale of a house or other disposing of property, the closing of a business. Generally family members will vent a lot of anger and frustration. This means you will do a lot of listening, and it can be quite unpleasant for you. You, however, may be a stabilizing force in that family member's life. You, now more than ever, need to be that city set upon the hill that could not be hid, and the salt of the earth (Matthew 5:13–16).

If the family recognizes your efforts with a gift, please be gracious and accept it. This is their manner of showing their appreciation for your efforts.

Chapter 16
Friend of a Suicide Victim

I was pouring my second cup of coffee when the phone rang. Answering it quickly to prevent the ring from waking my family, I heard the duty officer identify herself and say, "Petty Officer Jones received a call from home half an hour ago. His father committed suicide." I threw my uniform on and headed to my ship.

On my way to the ship, I reviewed what I knew about Petty Officer Jones. He was pretty much a loner, highly intelligent, very open about his beliefs, a great chess player (I never beat him), known as a hard worker. The loner part bothered me. He had little in the way of a support system as far as I knew. As I crossed the quarterdeck, the duty officer advised me that Petty Officer Smith was waiting for me in the ship's library.

"We have the duty driver taking him to the airport in about 20 minutes, Chaplain," she called after me as I entered the bowels of the vessel. That answered a question I hadn't asked yet.

Upon entering the library, I saw Petty Officer Jones had his bags packed and was ready to leave. He stood up and accepted my offered hand. "Hey, Chaps, thanks for coming in this early." His voice was very saddened and quiet.

"I'm really sorry to hear about your father," I said. "How are you doing?"

"I'm pretty confused. When I was home on leave a couple weeks ago, I could tell he was having problems, but didn't think it was anything this big." He had a distant look in his eyes as he recalled being on leave. "I've called him a couple times since and he didn't sound this bad."

"Listen, I know it's going to be hard for you to hear me on this," I began as I sat him down for a moment. "This is not your fault. You did the best you could from here."

"That's what my chief said," he replied softly. "I feel like there is more I could have done, but I don't know what it would have been."

"That's very common when someone has a family member or friend who does this." I sort of went "clinical" on him to give him something to consider on the way to the airport or on the plane ride, or hopefully both. "You want to think about what more you could have done, and the answer is probably 'nothing.'" I let that sink in for a moment before continuing. "You are a good son, you did all you could, and you did the best you could. You don't deserve to place a load of guilt on yourself." I knew it would take time for that to process.

We chatted a few more minutes until his chief arrived with his emergency leave papers. We then walked him to the quarterdeck where the duty driver was waiting to take him to the airport. My last words were for him to come see me as soon as he returned.

Surprisingly, two days later I was sitting in my office when I received a phone call from one of the corpsmen (my phone calls came through our ship's medical department), saying Petty Officer Jones wanted to speak to me. I became a little nervous wondering what he might be considering. As the call went through with the familiar clicking sounds I was wishing my assistant was not at a class, so I would have back up. Yet, all my worries were unfounded.

"Chaplain, do you remember what you told me in the library, about I did the best I could and I shouldn't blame myself?" Petty Officer Jones asked.

"Yes, I do remember that," I replied curiously.

"I'm sitting here with my mom, and she's having a hard time with this." I recalled hearing from him that his parents had been divorced for several years. "Would you please speak to her?" I could hear my shipmate coaxing his mother to take the phone and speak with me.

The words had been effective to him, and had already been passed on.

"Hi, Mrs. Jones, this is Chaplain Scott."

Her voice was soft and quiet. "Hi."

"Mrs. Jones, I'm very sorry for the loss of your husband. I understand you weren't still together, but his death is a loss, I know."

"Thank you."

"Are you blaming yourself for his death?"

The pause was deafening. "If I hadn't left him he might still be alive."

"But he might still have taken his life if you were still together. You couldn't have stopped him, babysat him twenty-four hours a day."

She didn't say anything, but I could hear her exhale.

"And Mrs. Jones, did you do everything you could to help your husband."

"I tried, I really tried."

"Then Mrs. Jones, his death is not your fault, not your fault at all."

We spoke a few more minutes, and she began understanding that the death of her ex-husband was not her fault. It takes a while for people to fully accept this.

UNDERSTANDING THE CRISIS

Being the friend or family member of a victim of suicide is, from what I have observed, the ultimate guilt-producing event. Nearly, if not all, of the family members and close friends go through serious guilt and experience the, "If only I had..." Often this leads to the break-up of families; divorce often resulting if a child was involved. Or the blame game happens, "If only you had..." becomes a vicious cycle, which again, destroys families and friendships.

The truth is that most people don't recognize the signs of an impending possible suicide and therefore aren't in a position to take preventive actions. Frequently, the signs of suicide are mistaken for something else, such as: depression, anger, disappointment, confusion, a brain-chemical imbalance, rebellion, or something along those lines.

Further, people plot their suicides carefully so that they can't be prevented from carrying through with it, and thus no one could have prevented it. At this time, the most important thing friends and family need to do is to draw together and mutually support one-another.

It is especially important that other family members be watched for signs of suicide. Family members of suicide victims, especially the children and siblings, are much more likely to attempt or commit suicide than other members of the population.

APPLICABLE SCRIPTURE

Come to me, all you who are weary and burdened, and I will give you rest.

—Matthew 11:28

I have told you these things, so that you may have peace. In this world you will have trouble. But take heart! I have overcome the world.

—John 16:33

My comfort in my suffering is this: Your promise preserves my life.

—Psalm 119:50

WHAT TO PRAY FOR

- Pray for the family to support one another.
- If the victim was a child, pray that the parents don't play the "blame game."
- Pray other family members don't contemplate suicide.
- Pray the family and friends receive the counseling and support needed to recover.

HOW TO HELP

This will be one of the most difficult situations for a non-professional (and for the professional) to be involved in. Family dynamics, deep-seated guilt, serious grief, and depression all make supporting a parishioner, friend or family suffering through this extremely difficult.

My first recommendation is for the family and friends to go to counseling. A trained pastor or therapist will be better suited to sort through the family dynamics, and will also be objective, rather than subjective due to family involvement. Your help may be critical in recommending a good counselor or pastoral professional.

People need reassureance through this as their guilt tends to eat at them, especially during alone time. They lose sleep, and usually don't eat or overeat. They let themselves go in other areas such as hygiene. If you notice this, bring it to their attention. Suggest they go for a physical exam. Their physician may recommend a sleeping aid to help them get rest, and may refer them for counseling if they aren't already going.

Encourage forgiveness. The family needs to forgive each other as well as forgive themselves. Forgiveness probably won't occur immediately, or even soon, but it needs to be encouraged, and dealt with. In some cases, forgiveness must extend to forgiving the person who committed suicide in order for the person or family to move on.

Schools, many government offices, hospitals, and many businesses bring in CISD (Critical Incident Stress Debriefing) teams after a student or co-worker commits suicide. This helps promote the grief and healing process. If you work where a co-worker commits suicide, I highly recommend contacting a local hospital, county mental health center, or even school to find out how to bring in a CISD team. I have been a team member as well as a recipient, and the results are phenomenal.

As with any family going through grief and shock, they would probably appreciate any help you would give in the form of meals, calls, lawn and yard work, and helps such as those.

Chapter 17
Friend of One Who is Dying

The ringing phone caught my attention as I entered the parsonage. I picked it up and could hear someone crying. "Hello?" I answered softly.

"Pastor Scott, this is Julie." Julie was a friend of my family and attended a church one street up from mine. I heard sorrow in her voice.

"Julie, what's the matter?" I questioned.

"It's Nancy. Her husband just called me. She has cancer and isn't expected to live much longer."

I was shocked. Nancy and her family lived at a fish hatchery on an island about a mile off the coast of our town in Alaskan. She was young, in her early thirties, and had three young kids, two the same age as ours. Every so often she motored into town in a small boat to shop and do laundry, and her kids would play with ours. She was a very pleasant person to be around. Everyone liked Nancy. Actually, everyone loved Nancy.

"Oh, Julie, I'm so sorry. Where is she?" She named a hospital in Anchorage. She also said she was calling as many pastors as possible to have their churches pray for Nancy and her family.

A few days later my wife and I flew to Anchorage and visited with Nancy. She was hooked to machines, IVs, and she didn't look anything like the Nancy we knew. We were told to keep our visit short.

"I am not afraid of dying, I know I am going to heaven," Nancy told us. "But I don't want to leave Mike and the kids without someone to care for them."

My wife and I reassured Nancy that God would take care of all of her family's needs.

After a few short minutes Nancy appeared exhausted and we left.

The next morning I called the hospital to talk to Nancy briefly to arrange a visit and the nursing supervisor advised us that she had experienced a rough night and asked us not to visit. We flew back to our town.

A few days later Julie called. As soon as I heard her voice I knew. "Pastor Scott," she said slowly and softly. "Nancy died early this morning." I just held the phone while she cried.

UNDERSTANDING THE CRISIS

Providing comfort to the dying is one of the most difficult and exhausting ministries. When someone dies unexpectedly in an accident, the ministry is to the family, grief is the emotion dealt with, and the family tends to pull together, trying to get along with their lives shortly thereafter (unless a child is involved).

When a person discovers they are terminally ill, the ministry is to that person, as well as to their family. If you are close to the family, you may find yourself being over taxed by the burden of ministering to both the terminally ill person and the family. The family really should be using someone they can go to for help to get through the process like a pastor, priest, or counselor.

Assuming that the terminally ill person is bedridden, your visits should be for that person. The reverse would be true if you are a friend of one of the family members rather than the terminally ill person. This chapter, though, will focus on ministry to the terminally ill.

In some cases you may find yourself in the middle of a dispute between family members, which could include (and most likely will) the terminally ill individual. I have heard of disputes regarding the turning off of life support equipment, cremation rather than burial, where to bury, and type of funeral. While your heart may be in the right place, unless you avoid the "middle ground," the situation will take a heavy toll on you.

At this point I would like to recommend two books: *On Death and Dying* by Elisabeth Kubler-Ross, and *Death and the Caring Community: Ministering to the Terminally Ill* by Larry Richards and Paul Johnson, M.D.

Elisabeth Kubler-Ross did the pioneer writing in the area of the emotional stages a terminally ill person experiences. Her five stages: denial and isolation, anger, bargaining, depression, and acceptance, were considered ground-breaking and have been taught in universities, seminaries, medical schools and self-help groups for decades.

Richards' and Johnson's book is written especially for those who are ministering to the terminally ill. Kubler-Ross primarily targets the medical community, and to a lesser degree clergy, Richards and Johnson targets clergy and family. They include much of Kubler-Ross' information in *Death and the Caring Community*. If you were to purchase only one book, I would recommend Richards' and Johnson's book.

One of the key points Richards and Johnson make is that the terminally ill generally fear dying more than they fear death. Among their many fears are: isolation, pain, desertion, helplessness, finances, being a burden, and many others. They also break down the major concerns of the terminally ill by age group and gender. The following chart is from their book [*Death and the Caring Community*; Multnomah Press: 1980 p. 48]:

Twenties

- leaving family they love

- how loved ones will cope with grief

- financial and emotional burden on loved ones

- lack of significant accomplishment

Thirties

- fear of pain

Forties

- welfare of the children and spouse

- financial security for survivors

- dread of separation

Fifties

- welfare of the family

- anxiety concerning drawn out death, personal suffering

- fear of being kept alive beyond hope of recovery

Women

- her abandonment of the children

- guilt feelings

- not living to see the children grow up

Men

- financial security of the family

- end of productivity

- loss of control

Other factors to be considered besides the fears of the patient you are ministering to are the desires of the person. Often this means setting aside your personal desires and beliefs (without compromising your faith). More will be said about this in the Procedures section, however, be aware that a person in extreme pain, or feeling isolated or hopeless, very well may make some decisions or statements concerning life support, medication, the location where they choose to die, financial arrangements, or a number of things which you may disagree with. Try not to argue with them and understand where they are coming from.

A final word here, you are likely to feel helpless and useless in this situation. You can't take away their pain. You can't extend their life or change their physical circumstances. You will probably wear down emotionally. *Be aware of that.* You are there for their spiritual well being.

WHAT TO PRAY FOR

- Pray for the salvation of the dying person if he/she isn't a Christian.

- Pray for comfort for the dying person.

- Pray for the dying person's family.

- Pray for the medical care providers, their jobs are difficult ones.

- Pray for your own spiritual and emotional strength.

APPLICABLE SCRIPTURE

For the terminally ill:

Precious in the sight of the LORD is the death of his saints.

—Psalm 116:15

I know that my Redeemer lives, and that in the end he will stand upon the earth. And after my skin has been destroyed, yet in my flesh I will see God; I myself will see him with my own eyes—I, and not another. How my heart yearns within me!

—Job 19:25–27

I will ransom them from the power of the grave, I will redeem them from death. Where, O death, are your plagues? Where, O grave, is your destruction?

—Hosea 13:14

All of 1 Corinthians 15, [The Resurrection chapter]

For the caregiver:

You are the salt of the earth. But if the salt has lost its saltiness, how can it be made salty again? It is no longer good for anything, except to be thrown out and trampled by men. You are the light of the world. A city on a hill cannot be hidden. Neither do people light a lamp and put it under a bowl. Instead they put it on its stand, and it gives light to everyone in the house. In the same way, let your light shine before men, that they may see your good deeds and praise your Father in heaven.

—Matthew 5:13–16

All of 1 Corinthians 13 [The love chapter]

HOW TO HELP

I can't stress enough how difficult this will be for you. However, I also can't stress how important this assignment actually is. While you may be asking yourself, "What does he mean by assignment?" I want to refer you to the first Bible verse in the preceding section. If in fact God views the death of one of His saints as precious, your participation and helping in the last period of her life is part of their preparation for being with Him. I would encourage you to look at what your are doing as a ministry to and for God, as well as for the patient.

Read and understand the five stages of the dying process which Kubler-Ross identified:

1. **Denial:** Refusing to believe or act upon the belief that they are dying.
2. **Anger:** Bitterness and frustration at being cut off from family and life.
3. **Bargaining:** Seeking to put off the end.
4. **Depression:** As the pain increased and the body weakens, depression sets in.
5. **Acceptance:** A readiness to die. Often after all resources to prolong life have been exhausted.

Not all terminally ill patients experience all five stages. Also, to a minor degree, patients may pass back and forth from one to another as they transition. The more you understand the more you will be able to communicate and help the terminally ill person.

If the terminally ill patient is a child, the parent(s) very well may go through the five stages themselves. If the child is very young, they may not. Parents tend to support heroic efforts to save children.

Try to listen without judging or arguing.

Try to be supportive without compromising your values.

Terminally ill patients appreciate company, and especially cherish someone who commits time to them on a regular basis. A few minutes can mean a lot. Even if you have nothing new to say, try to show the person you care by a few minutes of your presence.

Often if the terminally ill patient has lost much of their eyesight, or if they are too weak to old up a book, they may well appreciate having you read to them.

Pray with the person daily.

Don't neglect yourself or your family. This means physically and emotionally, as well as spiritually. Caring for a terminally ill person is extremely taxing. Make certain you maintain your prayer life, your family life, your church time, and get plenty of rest—physical and emotional. You can be very faithful without being a super hero and buring out. As a matter of fact, you can probably do more by limiting yourself to a daily or weekly basis.

The patient may be moved. They may go from one home to hospice to hospital, or make any number or combination of moves. Be prepared for their reactions to the changes, as well as to your reactions. Often the moves are against their will. Often their reactions are the result of feeling powerless.

The patient may come quite close to death one or more time(s) before they actually do die. This will probably take a high emotional toll on you.

After the patient dies, you will probably experience mixed emotions and very likely you will feel confused. The most common seems to be a sense of loss, and a sense of relief, which causes feelings of guilt. The guilt should pass soon, but if it doesn't, and if guilt becomes the predominant feeling sit down with your pastor or a counselor and discuss it.

Above all, remember how important this ministry is to the patient, and to God.

Chapter 18
Suicide/Suicidal Gestures

Jerked suddenly from a deep sleep I woke with a start and sat bolt upright in bed. It was shortly after 2:00 AM. Standing and glancing around the bedroom, I pictured clearly in my mind a man dressed in jeans, rubber boots, a heavy sweater and jacket, talking in a phone booth down on the waterfront in our fishing town. My wife awoke, "What are you doing?" she asked groggily.

"I'm not sure. I believe God woke me up. There's someone down by the Anchor Bar that needs help."

"You just have to go down there," she said confidently.

That's what I was thinking, too, so I finished dressing and drove down to the docks. Upon my arrival a man exactly as I envisioned was talking on the pay phone. I parked next to the booth to wait for him to finish his call. He dropped the phone and approached my car.

He was a forlorn looking soul, and I could smell alcohol on his breath. "Are you waiting for the phone?"

I looked him in the eye, "No, I told him," "I came here to talk to you."

He became pale and took on a startled expression. "To talk to me? Man, I don't know you, and you don't know me!"

"I know," I replied. "It's difficult to explain. I was asleep and God woke me up and told me to come and talk to you."

He looked even more startled than before. "God did what? He asked you to come to me?" Looking back at the phone booth he took a deep breath and said, "I'm talking to my wife. Can you wait a few minutes?" I nodded as I yawned.

He went back to the phone, picked up the handset and said, "Hey, I gotta go. Some guy here says God sent him down to talk to me."

I waited while he completed the call to his wife. Five minutes later, the dejected man sat silently in my car. I introduced myself to him as I drove toward my church.

"Why did you come down to the dock?" he questioned.

I repeated the truth to him. "I think God sent me to you."

"My wife didn't call you?" he asked.

"No, why would she have?"

"Because I told her I was going to jump off the docks to kill my-self." His voice was distant, as if he was talking to himself. In our fishing town in Alaska the water temperature was about 36° F at that time of year, meaning near instant coma, and then death.

I drove Richard to the church's kitchen and we spoke for several hours while eating breakfast and drinking coffee. He seemed to feel much better and saw hope for his future. I made some appointments for him to return for "chats" (many of the men seem reluctant to come in for "counseling" but they are willing to come in for "chats").

UNDERSTANDING THE CRISIS

Suicide affects families of all races, religions, economic status—everyone. No one group is exempt. Some people are more prone to commit suicide, but know that everyone is at risk.

People attempt or commit suicide for a number of reasons. Generally though, it is because they are experiencing intense emotional or physical pain, they are acting out of desperation because they feel overwhelmed by their circumstances, or they are severely depressed. As one Marine Corps Master Gunnery Sergeant told me when we were stationed on Okinawa, "Suicide is a permanent solution to a temporary problem."

People who plan to commit suicide leave signs or hints of what they are thinking. Some common indicators of an impending suicide are giving away possessions, withdrawal from friends or coworkers, reading or listening to morbid or depressing material, making statements such as, "The world will be a better place without me," or to that affect.

There is a vast difference between making a suicidal ideation and a suicidal gesture. This is based on the level of severity, but I want to emphasize that both need to be taken seriously. A suicidal ideation, in simplistic terms, is some vocalizing the thought of suicide. Often this is thought of as an attention getting device. Remember, though, it does demand your attention. Don't ignore it, don't disregard it, and try not to let it panic you.

A suicidal gesture, in simplistic terms, is someone taking action. This could be the person obtaining a weapon or a tool (rope, hoarding medication, etc.), or going to a cliff or bridge. It falls short of him/her making an attempt, but it means their process is moving in that direction. At this point you need to be obtaining professional help for the person if you haven't done so already, and if you are capable of doing so.

APPLICABLE SCRIPTURE

There is no commandment, which states, "Thou shalt not commit suicide." However since suicide is the murder of oneself, I consider Exodus 20:13 applicable. It reads simply, "You shall not murder."

In 1 Samuel 31:1–6 Saul is wounded in battle and surrounded by his enemies. He requests his armor bearer to kill him, but the poor fellow would not do it. Saul, therefore, committed suicide, as did his armor bearer after watching Saul.

Samson committed suicide by causing the roof of the Philistine temple to give way and crash down on himself and 3,000 Philistines (Judges 16).

In Matthew 27:5 we are told that Judas hanged himself after betraying Jesus.

In all three cases the men involved had rejected their calling by God, become defiant toward God, and were living sinful lives.

The most applicable Scriptures are those which give hope and promise of help to both you and the person in need. The Bible is filled with verses of hope and help; I will give just a few of my favorites here.

> I have told you these things, so that in me you may
> have peace. In this world you will have trouble. But
> take heart! I have overcome the world.
> —John 16:33

> For God did not give us a spirit of timidity, but a spirit
> of power, of love and of self-discipline.
> —2 Timothy 1:7

No temptation has seized you except what is common to man. And God is faithful; he will not let you be tempted beyond what you can bear. But when you are tempted, he will also provide a way out so that you can stand up under it.

—1 Corinthians 10:13

I can do everything through him who gives me strength.

—Philippians 4:13

O LORD my God, I called to you for help and you healed me.

—Psalm 30:2

WHAT TO PRAY FOR

Prayer is essential here, yet when you become aware of a suicidal person you are likely to be shocked by the situation. There have been many times when I have been confronted by this situation and I have taken the person's hand saying, "Let me pray for guidance now, if you don't mind." I pray out loud, and often the prayer helps the person become calm. If you can, pray "with" the individual rather than "for" the individual, using words such as "we" rather than third person words (i.e. him, her).

- Pray for God to strengthen and guide both of you.
- Pray for the Holy Spirit to anoint you with the words to say.
- Pray for peace to take the place of the pain or desperation in the suicidal person.
- If emergency responders are en-route, pray for them to arrive quickly.

HOW TO HELP

No situation is scarier to the average person than to be confronted by a suicidal person. Do not let your fear override your ability to think clearly. This person's life depends on your clear head.

If the person confronting you is making suicidal ideation, or if you think they may be making suicidal ideation, confront them. Bluntly ask them if he/she is thinking of harming himself/herself. Many people are reluctant to do this as they mistakenly believe that if the person isn't considering doing so then a seed to commit suicide will be planted in the person's mind. This is not the case. Many times when I've done this and was correct (about eighty-five to ninety percent of the time) the person look relieved to be asked, and it started the healing process.

In the cases of those not considering suicide, not one made an attempt because I planted a seed.

If the person responds that he/she is contemplating suicide I strongly recommend you get them to a professional counselor, therapist, or treatment facility that can help him/her deal with these feelings. The route I recommend is through the nearest emergency room. I recommend this for two reasons. First, once the treatment starts, even with the taking of vital signs, the person often feels that the helping process has begun. Secondly, a hospital emergency room can provide a psychologist or psychiatrist much quicker than you can.

Does this mean I am against a minister or priest intervening? No, it does not. A minister or priest can be brought in later. However, valuable time can be lost trying to track one down.

If you choose not to go through the emergency room, please stay with the person while you track down a trained professional. In the military everyone is taught to remain with the person while walking them to the chaplain or medical facility, or while waiting for the chaplain or medical professional to arrive.

If the person is making suicidal gestures *don't leave* unless the person is holding a weapon. If the person is holding a weapon, *withdraw* to a safe distance or location.

Attempt to communicate with the person. Listen to what they say. Try not to argue with them as this may increase their frustration. Try to give them encouragement and hope. Not only are you stalling while awaiting the arrival of emergency responders, you may be de-escalating the situation. Often suicidal people feel desperation in believing no one cares. If you show you care you may capture their attention. Don't lie to the person or make any promises you cannot keep. You are building trust, and if the person determines they cannot count on that trust it may cause the situation to escalate. Honesty is important.

Make every effort to call 911 or the appropriate emergency contact number. If possible send someone else to call and guide the emergency responders to the correct location. When calling the operator give as much detail as possible. (Most locations now have technology so if 911 is dialed and the phone is put down, the locale of the emergency can be detected immediately). Cars with Onstar and like services can be used as well.

If you are able to safely remove non-weapon devices (rope, medications, flame producing devices, etc.) do so, but try not to put yourself at risk. If you are injured in the attempt, the person may feel more desperate than they already are.

Again, it is recommended that the person receive medical attention. At a later time a minister or priest may be called in. I have been to visit a person on the following day after I was called in to intervene, and I was amazed at how much better they appeared and sounded after a good night's sleep. Did this preclude me from ministering to the person? Not at all, it just delayed it until the person was more rational.

If you encounter a suicidal person over the phone *don't hang up* unless they are so close you can run to them within a few seconds. Get someone else's attention and have them call 911 or the appropriate number. With your telephone number emergency personnel can trace the source of the call. Again, this is now the case with cellular phones and Onstar.

FOLLOW UP

I maintained contact with Rich, initially on a nearly daily basis. Several weeks after first encountering him down on the dock his wife called to thank me for intervening. At the end of the commercial fishing season he went back home to be with her, and I saw him again the following spring.

Other Issues

Chapter 19
Financial Crisis/Debt

I was quickly stepping out of my office on my way to watch our ship docking after being at sea for three weeks when a sailor caught up to me and stated he had to talk to me right away. We moved to an unoccupied area of the main deck and he cast his gaze down towards his steel-toed boots. "Chaps, my wife and I are about to go bankrupt. We need help badly."

"How close are you?" I questioned.

"I spoke to my wife on the phone when we were in port last week. She said a towing company was trying to schedule to repossess her car."

"Can you two come see me and bring your bills tomorrow?" I asked.

"I don't think so, Sir. But if you'd be willing to come to our house, we live in base housing." He nearly pleaded with me.

"Sure thing, it's Saturday, so it won't be a problem." I generally try to spend the weekends after being at sea or in the field (with Marines) with family, but this was a serious situation. Going into serious debt in the military or in many government jobs can cause a person to lose their security clearance.

I arrived at their home at 9:00 AM the next morning. Upon my arrival I noted two fairly new cars in front of the home. When I was welcomed into the home I saw a lot of "toys" in the way of a big-screen television, nice stereo, cell phones and things like that. As we sat down and looked at the couple's bills verses their income, they had more outgo each month than they had income. Their credit card bills were killing them, along with their car payments.

"Our parents used to help us pay our bills, but now they won't do that anymore," the sailor advised me.

"I can understand that," I responded. "You need to learn to live within your income."

"What do we do about the creditors?" The wife asked.

"You have to sell some of your possessions to generate money. I don't see any other way around it." I stood and walked into the living room.

"Like what?" The wife asked.

"I'd start with the TV and stereo. I'd get rid of at least one cell phone, and also one of the cars."

"What will we do without a TV?" She asked.

"You can perhaps get one; it just won't be as big."

"And my car, I use it to get to work and to shop when he's at work." She viewed her desire for "things" ahead of living within her income.

"It's not going to be as convenient using one car, and having to take the bus or ride a bike, but the creditor is already planning to take your car."

The reality of losing possessions finally began to dawn on them. I also set them up with a non-profit consumer counseling service, which works with creditors to help individuals, and families overcome debt.

UNDERSTANDING THE CRISIS

Debt is spending more than you're making. As simple as it sounds, that is what is happening when a family or individual goes into debt. Sometimes it happens due to a crisis such as when a home catches on fire, or a flood happens, the loss of employment, but from my observations the vast majority of serious debt is the result of overextending credit. It happens to people at all levels of income, age brackets, races, and to both individuals as well as families.

A further observation is that debt seems to "sneak up" on a lot people. They don't seem to be aware of what they are spending per month compared with what their monthly income and expenses are. Monthly expenses are reoccurring expenses such as rent, food, utilities, etc. When credit payments are added to reoccurring expenses and the total approaches net income (income after taxes, social security, and other deductions) then a serious problem is facing the couple. That means there likely isn't an emergency fund, a retirement fund, or education fund for the children. If the family is renting, very likely money isn't being set aside for the purchase of a home.

All too often, as in the above scenario, the debt results from the credit being used to purchase luxury items. "Wants" gets confused with "needs," and the thought of denying the pleasure of a luxury item seems to be more than one can bear. Many people attempt to blame credit card companies, salespeople, even advertising, but the overall responsibility rests of the people who do the spending.

As in the above scenario, parents or other family members bail the debtors out. Generally, though, this leads to further debt, and when the gift-income is spent, there seems to be more debt than before. Bailing people out also tends to develop a staving off of learning responsibility, resentment, and codependency issues.

APPLICABLE SCRIPTURE

The wicked borrow and do not repay.

—Psalm 37:21

A greedy man brings trouble to his family.

—Proverbs. 15:27

The borrower is servant to the lender.

—Proverbs. 22:7b

WHAT TO PRAY FOR

- Pray for wisdom to teach them sound financial planning, or find a teacher.

- If you gave/loaned money, pray for understanding to stop this practice.

- Pray for them to soundly rebound from debt.

- Pray for them to understand the difference between needs and wants.

- If additional employment is necessary, pray for the right job(s)

HOW TO HELP

I am not a great financial genius, so I generally refer people in serious debt to a non-profit consumer credit counselor. Often an agency has established relationships with many of the credit agencies and is able to work out a program to help the debtor(s) repay without a heavy penalty.

An alternative is to have the family approach their bank or credit union for a consolidation loan, or perhaps a home equity loan. These are not easy to obtain if the debt load is high, and may take days to acquire.

If the debtor(s) is/are not on a budget, then it will be necessary to help them develop one. As many expenses as possible need to be taken into consideration, and often a month after the initial budget is developed, a meeting to tweak the budget should take place to add expenses missed in the first budget meeting. Extravagant lifestyles need to be examined and if necessary, tamed. People who eat fancy foods, indulge in alcohol or tobacco, have cable or satellite TV, play lottery or otherwise gamble, go to professional sporting events, or waste money in various other ways need to be taught money discipline.

Often the debtors need to hold a garage or yard sale to sell unnecessary possessions to make money to pay bills. Another option is to advertise in the newspaper, which generally brings more money. Selling through a pawnshop earns the least money.

Advise people not to take out "Payday loans" as they have outrageous interest rates and cause further into debt.

Debtor(s) should be made to destroy all credit cards. If they refuse, walk away from the situation. In fact, run away.

If the individual/couple has time, encourage them to seek additional income. Even if it's low paying, it will still help eliminate their debt. If they decline due to laziness or pride, run away. If they won't make the effort to get out of debt, why should you?

People who have suffered from natural disasters or job loss need help of a different sort. They may need counseling to help them through their losses, as well as a new job, housing, clothing, appliances, transportation, and more. Often insurance takes longer than expected, and offerings of various helps may be needed to tide people over. People should not be penalized for what they could not help.

Encourage people to set aside money for emergencies. Most financial planners and counselors recommend six months worth of "liquid" assets. "Liquid" means cash or savings rather than land or something difficult to cash in.

I always encourage Christian couples to tithe, as our faithfulness to God is rewarded (Malachi 3:6–10). Use resources. There are many books written by Christian and non-Christian authors on sound financial living. They include instruction on budgeting, getting out of debt, investing, even shopping at a grocery store or buying a car. Some authors I have read are Ron Blue and Malcolm MacGregor. There are also some excellent video series that give some of the same instruction.

Try to utilize a non-profit consumer counselor. Often the couple's bank or credit union has someone. Be wary of the for-profit companies that advertise on TV. Within the military the Family Service Centers have trained and experienced personnel to help. Each service's aid society often has financial counseling.

Chapter 20
Loss of Employment

Case #1

Our ship pulled in after being at sea for five weeks. I stood out on the starboard (right) deck, gazing at the majestic mountains and serene islands as we turned toward our homeport. Suddenly I was aware of a sailor standing next to me.

"Chaps, I have a problem and I don't know what to do." He continued looking at the peaks as he spoke.

"Do you want to go to my office and talk, or do you want to stay out here?"

Without answering my question, he turned and faced me. "My father-in-law has been staying at my house for four months now, ever since he lost his job, and he doesn't seem motivated to go get a new job."

We both leaned against the bulkhead.

"He was a sheet metal fabricator," he continued, "but the company he worked for shut down. He didn't get much money out of his retirement plan."

"Has he been out looking for work at all?"

"Not too much. He's in his late fifties, and most companies want younger employees. Some of the work he did can be done by machines now. He'd need to start a whole new career."

"Is he willing to start a new career? I know it is generally difficult for an older person to start a new career all over again."

"He says he is, but frankly, computers scare him. He's much better working with his hands. But at his age, and with back problems, I don't know what to expect of him."

"I imagine he's getting frustrated going from place to place," I said, "having doors slammed in his face, being told he is too old or not qualified."

"Right, that's what he's said, and he has great work ethic."

"That's probably a lot of his frustration. Knowing he has a great work ethic and having people probably younger than he is telling him he's under-qualified, or that there isn't any work for him, has to hurt."

"What do I do, Chaplain?"

"Listen to him. Don't try to push him to learn computers if he's afraid of them." I knew how hard this sailor he pushed himself, and I had a feeling he had been pushing his father-in-law.

"Just listen to him?"

"If you listen, it allows him to voice his frustrations—to get it all out. Once his frustration is out, then it allows him to focus on what he needs to do."

"So I don't need to encourage him, or motivate him?" the sailor looked surprised.

"People his age are motivated differently. You might actually discourage him, if he thinks you believe he doesn't want to work." I let that sink in for a moment. "Where is your mother-in-law in all this?"

"They divorced a long time ago. He never remarried."

"He's looking to your family for comfort and companionship." By his expression, I could tell he understood what I was saying. "When you get back home today, just listen to him and let him know you understand. If he asks you for help, then give it to him. Remember, he's worked hard all his life. That is where a large portion of his self-worth and value to others lie."

Case #2

I zipped up my jacket and grabbed my briefcase. One of my students asked to see me.

"What seems to be wrong?" I asked.

"It's about my husband," she said. "He did his four years in the Air Force and got out about four or five months ago. Since then he just sits at home playing video games—all day long. That's what he does, play video games." She looked frustrated.

"Does he have any plans to find work or go to school?" I knew from previous classes that she didn't have any children, so he wasn't babysitting.

"He says he does, though when I ask him what his plans are—he's vague about it." She slumped down into a chair. "I'm only an E-4. I had hopes of getting out at the end of the year and going to college full time."

"But if he won't get a job that ruins your plans?"

"It sure does, it ruins it big-time. I want to do ROTC and come back in the Air Force as an officer, but my husband is using up our savings."

"How is it getting used?" I asked.

"He bought a home theater system last month—that cost $3,000.00. He also bought a new video camera and a motorcycle."

"He's healthy and capable of working?"

"Oh yes, he's quite healthy."

"Is he willing to go for some counseling?"

"Job counseling?"

"Marriage counseling. This situation sounds like its affecting your marriage."

"I haven't thought of it like that. I'll ask him."

I wrote the telephone number for the Air Force chaplain's office so she could call them the next day. When I dismissed my class two evenings later, the Air Force woman remained seated. I started to approach her when a man came and stood in the doorway.

"May I help you?" I asked him.

"I heard you were willing to talk to me," he replied.

"He's my husband," the woman spoke from where she sat. "I asked him to meet us here. He wasn't willing to go to the chaplain's office as you suggested."

The young man (about twenty-three years old) slumped into a nearby chair. "So what did you want to talk about?" he asked.

"Your wife seems upset that you won't find work, and that you are using family savings to make big purchases."

A look of shock appeared on his face. "You told him that?" he said in a barely controlled voice. "Why would you tell some college teacher that?"

"He's also a chaplain."

"I'd like to hear what you have to say," I said trying to regain control of the conversation.

"There aren't any jobs out there I really want. I thought I'd wait until we got back to the U.S. in a few months to try and work."

"What are you going to do in the meantime?"

"I don't know. Hanging out I guess." He didn't seem comfortable with the answer.

I looked at his wife. "Is that acceptable to you?"

She seemed surprised by the question. "No, it's not acceptable. And neither is the wild spending."

"What would be mutually acceptable to both of you?"

"I don't know if there is anything that would make us both happy," the man shrugged. "As long as she's got pay coming in, we're doing okay."

"You're not doing okay. Your behavior is upsetting your wife."

"What's wrong with not working for a while?"

"Well, since you asked," I began, "the Bible teaches that if a man will not work then neither is he to be provided for. Idleness and laziness are both against biblical principles." I let him think on that for a moment.

"Deciding not to work is something you should discuss with your wife before you do it," I continued. "Besides, if you allow your wife to support you like this, you will turn her into a codependent and an enabler, supporting someone whose lifestyle she doesn't agree with. Is that what you want to do?"

He slumped further down into the chair. "Well, no."

UNDERSTANDING THE CRISIS

There are many reasons why people end up losing their jobs: forced retirement for age or medical reasons, layoff or firing, job source going out of business or reorganization and many other reasons. In many cases, work is found soon after a job loss, or if not, in a fairly reasonable period of time. For those, a crisis doesn't occur.

But for those who don't find work soon, it may turn into a crisis situation for them and their family. As illustrated by the previous true scenarios, there are two primary responses from people out of work for an extended period of time. We will look at situations where it turns into a crisis or near crisis situation.

Technological advancements and achievements enhance the lives of many in developed countries. Computers and computer-enhanced machinery make production of many items cheaper, quicker, and more precise; allowing, in many cases, a longer lifespan for the product.

However, for the hands on craftsman, computer assisted work is a threat. It means the possibility of being replaced by machines and losing livelihood. If and when that time comes, employers will look for someone with technological skills.

A person with a strong work ethic, an excellent work history, and a desire to work doesn't like being told he/she is no longer a desirable worker. They experience hurt, anger, and confusion, and a boatload of disappointment. (Why would someone rather have something made by a machine rather than by a skilled artisan?)

There is often a fear of the technology, which seems to be invading their world. Something not understood is something unknown. Something unknown is something to be feared.

This fear of technology coupled with age, even in mid-life, makes it difficult for a person to be hired in many companies and government agencies. It's not a question of the job seeker desiring to work; it's not having the right skills for the job.

The second scenario presents an entirely different situation. Found primarily between high school students up to people in their late 20's, the prevailing attitude here is that menial, low paying or low technology jobs are beneath them, and it's better to not work at all than to do jobs lacking "dignity." Business owners and supervisors tell me that people with little or no work history come to them and try to dictate pay, hours, and working conditions—as if they are skilled experienced workers.

Recently a couple came to me for counseling. Their primary concern was getting rid of debt so the wife could afford to go to college. When I asked if she had any job prospects she replied to the effect, "No, all that's been offered to me is housekeeping at a nursing home and convenience store work."

"Which did you take?" I inquired.

"Well, neither."

"Why not?" I questioned, surprised by her response.

"I don't want to be a cleaning lady or a cashier."

"Why not? It is honest work and you could be paying off your bills right now."

"I want something that pays better, and is better work."

"How old are you?"

"I'm twenty."

"And how experienced of a worker are you?"

"Well, I'm not. I've only been a student."

Her husband sat nodding his head, then took her hand, and said, "Honey, maybe you ought to go back to the nursing home and see if the housekeeping job is still open."

Honest work of any sort is not beneath anyone's dignity.

Another matter to consider in the second scenario, are people who work a job for a short while and then purposely get themselves fired to collect unemployment benefits. If they quit their job, they collect nothing. Not only do they collect benefits from the government, but their family generally ends up supporting them as well. Their family, as a unit, unwittingly becomes a codependent enabler. Essentially, a person refusing to work is telling those around him/her, "I expect you to support me."

APPLICABLE SCRIPTURE

For those who choose not to work:

> In the name of the Lord Jesus Christ, we command you, brothers, to keep away from every brother who is idle and does not live according to the teaching you received from us. For you yourselves know how you ought to follow our example. We were not idle when we were with you, nor did we eat anyone's food without paying for it. On the contrary, we worked night and day, laboring and toiling so that we would not be a burden to any of you. (Paul was a tentmaker even while an apostle.) We did this, not because we did not have the right to such help, but in order to make ourselves a model to you to follow. For even when we were with you, we gave you this rule: "If a man will not work, he shall not eat."
>
> —2 Thessalonians 3:6–10

> Lazy hands make a man poor, but diligent hands bring wealth. He who gathers crops in the summer is a wise son, but he who sleeps during harvest is a disgraceful son.
>
> —Proverbs 10:4–5

WHAT TO PRAY FOR

- Pray for God's provision of work.

- Pray for those working for companies going through financial difficulty and layoffs.

- Pray for the family members of people choosing not to work.

- Pray for patience in helping those seeking work.

HOW TO HELP

For helping an older person who lost their job, your position is one of support. Supporting them involves listening to them and helping them look for work. Depending upon the person you're helping, you may suggest taking classes to learn new skills.

Older people, especially men, who have had the same job, or worked for the same company for decades, find their identity is often wrapped up in their work. Therefore, to them losing their job is losing their identity—and often their self-worth.

Men in their fifties, sixties, and beyond find their value and self-worth tied to "bringing home the bacon." A man *works* to provide for his family. A successful man provides well for his family. A highly successful man provides very well for his family. Therefore a man who isn't working is not a good provider.

Helping a man with this type of work ethic can be difficult. For one thing, he may not respect anyone who doesn't work as much as he has or who is not the kind of provider he has been. If judgment appears, back off.

If, however, he listens to you, appeal to his sense of self-worth. Help him understand that his worth involves his identity in Christ. Further, point out his efforts and success at being a husband and a father provide a valuable sense of worth. It is essential he understands this concept—otherwise his retirement years are bound to be short and miserable.

A wonderful book for men concerning this topic is *The Worth of a Man* by Dave Dravecky (Zondervan, 1996). Dravecky was a pitcher for a professional baseball team. At a fairly young age during the height of his career, he lost his pitching arm and shoulder to cancer. He explains his struggle to recover emotionally and spiritually from the loss, and he shares his gain in perspective on the real worth of a man.

While the out-of-work person scans the newspaper and hits the streets looking for a job, you can put the word out to your family, friends, and church that an honest and hard working person is looking for work. People are often hired from word-of-mouth advertising, especially where a hard worker is concerned. When an employer anticipates a personnel loss, they may hire someone based on a good reference rather than hire someone else off the street, even if it means hiring the recommended person early.

However, when helping someone who refuses to work, is looking for "the perfect job," or who purposely gets fired to collect benefits, I would advise against this, as it could ruin a helper's reputation.

In dealing with a person who refuses to work or hold a steady job, my recommendation would be the same as for anyone in a codependent enabling situation—*stop the enabling behavior.* Once the support system stops, then either the behavior changes or the person packs up and takes his behavior elsewhere. Eventually they will run out of people to pull their scam on and have to face reality.

I have counseled several parents, grandparents, and spouses who have been victimized by children, grandchildren or spouses who either won't work, or purposely get fired. This behavior causes a lot of heartache for families. If the person refusing to work is a parent, it sets a poor example the children and proves to be an embarrassment for them. My counsel is nearly always the same, stop supporting them, and if they are living in your home ask them to leave. I also recommend counseling for families who are caught in this trap. These families often feel guilt, that it was their poor parenting that caused the behavior, but that is most often not the case. Further, they feel that if they stop their support and ask the child to leave, it is bad parenting, which is also not the case. In fact, it is responsible parenting.

This does not apply to those who are unable to work due to health or health of others they are caring for, the retired, and parents who stay home to raise children.

ADDITIONAL INFORMATION

Financial planners and advisers recommend that all families and individuals insulate themselves against the affects of a job loss with a ninety-day cash reserve. This is money readily available to pay bills in the event you lose your job. I asked a friend of my family, Corrie Moore, a professional financial advisor my wife and I use, to submit the following:

Emergency Money and Developing Your Spending Plan

First, I'd like to take this opportunity to extend many thanks to clergyman, author, counselor, and chaplain, Lonnie Scott. When I first experienced Lonnie's passion for helping others, it really impressed upon me the miracle of the human spirit and our ability to give of ourselves.

Lonnie asked me to address the importance of having adequate cash reserves and protection in the case of unforeseen negative changes to either your income (i.e. job loss, job change, demotion, disability, death) or expenses (i.e. auto repairs, medical expenses, leaky roof). I find it difficult to jump into rules of thumb about how much is enough for an emergency fund and why it's important without touching on the fundamental concepts of cash flow.

Whether we admit it or not, we all have a spending plan. Make no mistake; not having a plan *is* a plan. Some people meticulously itemize each expense in a given month and can tell you to the penny exactly how much they spent on toilet paper last year. However, the majority of us operate on a less structured version ranging from a pile of ATM receipts to balancing our check register against our bank statements every month. Wherever you fall along the spectrum, my first recommendation is "Don't beat yourself up!" This does not excuse you from needing to understand how the cash flows through your household.

I'm here to tell you that we are all individuals and the best system is the one that works for you, because that's the one you'll use! Whichever system you decide to incorporate, it is essential that it include these basics:

1. **Before Tax Income** This allows you to account for all of the "deductions" automatically being pulled out of your paycheck before you see it. I've found it is helpful for clients to see on a monthly basis how much of their hard-earned dollars they never see. Deductions can include taxes, medical premiums, insurance premiums, automatic bank draft payments to loans or other obligations, pre-tax flex plan payments for childcare and medical expanses (offered through some employers). Payroll systems vary from weekly to monthly. People who are paid twenty-six times per year may be tempted to view two of their paychecks each year as "bonus" or "extra" checks. This can be helpful in "finding" the resources to start a savings or investment plan.

2. **Fixed Income** (rental property, child support, school stipend) It's easy to forget to include these sources of income, but important to recognize and account for them.

3. **Fixed Expenses** Monthly or annual expenditures which tend to stay the same. This includes mortgage, auto payments (e.g. boat, vacation home), insurance premiums (medical/life/ auto/home), professional or union dues, systematic savings or investment plans (retirement contributions pre or post tax),

membership dues (clubs/ hobbies/ organizations), Internet service fees, childcare, tuition, etc.

4. **Variable Expenses** Monthly or annual expenditures that fluctuate. They include taxes (income/ property), utilities (power/ water/ gas/ garbage), auto maintenance and gasoline, groceries, personal care items and services, clothing, household items and services, medical and prescription co-payments, home improvement, furniture and major appliances, education and professional development, debt/installment payments, entertainment, dining out, vacations, charitable contributions, jewelry, collectibles, gifts.

To begin, you'll want to gather all of the documents, which will supply the numbers you need to get started (checkbook, ATM receipts, credit card receipts, billing statements, bank statements, pay stubs, retirement and investment statements). This can be overwhelming your first time, but once its altogether, you will be amazed at how much easier it is to keep up with (binders or folders or trays are helpful for organizing between reviews).

Once you have a system in place, it's best to start this process at the beginning of each year, with your first paycheck. However, if it's your first time, it is very difficult to retroactively create your history showing past cash flow (at least six months) so that you can find out where your money has been going each month. Were you ahead or behind? Did you realize that your average visit to the cash machine is costing you $100 and you're going around three times a month?

The sense of empowerment this one act provides is worth a few hours over a weekend. I recommend couples do this together regardless of who normally "handles" the money. I guarantee it will be well worth your time.

The act of putting the dollars in writing can be accomplished by hand or automated. The manual version can be done by using a plain piece of paper and a pen. Grid lines are helpful for creating a table, but other than that, the format is irrelevant. Spreadsheets are designed to do this kind of analysis and make it easier to pull totals, averages, and percentages. You can buy software, which is already programmed for "budgeting" or checking account management or you can build your own spreadsheet. Format and method are not important. The importance lies in just doing it.

Once you have transferred the totals onto one central report, you'll be able to see both general and specific information. It will also allow you to recognize trends in spending of which you might not have been aware. This exercise is essential to establishing an appropriate target for your rainy day fund. If you don't know what's coming in versus what's going out, there is no way of knowing what is left over. These "left-overs" are the key to accomplishing any financial goal you have—including emergency funds.

Hopefully, you have a positive number at the bottom of your cash flow analysis. If not, don't get discouraged! You now have the opportunity to make informed decisions about your spending plan to positively impact that number. Doesn't it feel good to be proactive instead of reactive?

Everyone should have a pool of funds, which is readily available without penalty (liquid) to meet emergency and other highly urgent, short-term needs. This pool is sometimes referred to as your "cash-reserves." The ideal size of your pool might need to be larger or smaller:

- Job Security/ Income Stream (variable vs. steady)/Industry Volatility
- Condition/Age of home, auto's and other substantial, necessary assets
- Health of you and your family/Ability to increase deductibles for reduced premiums/Limitations to health plan coverage and changing levels of benefit provided by employer (if at all)/ Number of children
- Your credit rating/Debt-to-income ratio/Spending habits
- Economic Conditions in your community (local business, cost of living, prevailing wages)
- Your temperament (conservative versus aggressive)
- Life events including Marriage/Buying a home/Pregnancy/ Adoption/ Starting your own business/Ageing parents/Kids in college/Retirement/ Long –term care/Illness/Disability/Death

In order to determine the appropriate level of cash flow analysis. Are they steady throughout the year or are there certain months where your spending fluctuates? Are you already saving part of your income on a systematic basis? How much are your total annual expenses divided by twelve?

Let's start with the assumption that you need to have between three and six months of expenses on hand. Write your number down.

How close are you to having this amount saved? If you are significantly short, you should consider reducing your spending while implementing a systematic savings plan. Remember, these dollars are your main protection against financial disaster.

Although it is tempting to consider credit cards as "emergency funds," I advise doing this only with extreme caution. Credit comes with a price and in most cases only compounds the problem with interest charges, late payment fees and possibly permanent damage to your credit rating.

After all, if your income goes away and you are forced to charge your monthly living expenses, how long until it becomes a worse problem than it was to begin with? How long will you continue to pay the price for not setting aside a small portion of your paycheck every month? It could be for the next seven to ten years or longer.

Let's consider some of my clients' situations relative to our three to six month guideline:

Joe is a sales rep for a local company. He is paid on commissions and has very few benefits. As a young bachelor, he has limited expenses, relative to his income. He rents an apartment and owns his own vehicle. He has good spending habits and discretionary income to put towards his goals.

Even though Joe doesn't have excessive financial responsibilities, he does have fluctuating income. Joe needs more in his pool to cover slow times in his industry, when his commissions are less.

He also must consider the out of pocket expenses associated with funding his own medical expenses. Joe covers his risk of becoming disabled by obtaining disability protection. Joe ensures his success by implementing an automatic investment plan to fund both his emergency pool and his retirement pool.

As Joe gets older, his circumstances change. He and I evaluate his progress towards his goals each year and make any adjustments necessary.

Travis and Becky plan their first child. He has a steady position with the state including full medical and retirement benefits and she works for a local healthcare organization.

Becky intends to take some time off after their child is born and wants to try opening her own private practice after that. They plan to have significantly longer than six months of expenses on hand. They anticipate the double hit of losing her income (temporarily) and increasing expenses (babies cost more).

They begin early by gradually decreasing their monthly expenses to adjust to living on just his income.

At the same time, they put the difference into their emergency fund to reach their goal of ten to twelve months in cash reserves. They cover their new family with additional life insurance to protect against the possibility of the unthinkable. They experience the joys of parenthood knowing they are prepared for any financial situation.

Becky is able to focus solely on motherhood and family fulfillment until she decides it is time to begin building her own practice. She has the financial cushion to dedicate herself to her business venture without concern about not being immediately profitable.

They meet with me annually to track their progress and make adjustments. Becky's prudent financial habits translate well into running her own business and she applies many of these same strategies to protect her corporate bottom line.

Karen is a school teacher. She is very close to retirement and has done a great job of planning for it. She has very little debt with the exception of her mortgage and a new vehicle. Karen is relatively certain about the level of her retirement income. It will cover her current expenses.

However, she will lose medical benefits when she quits teaching. She works with me to build a cash reserve that will cover out-of-pocket expenses for medical care, as well as deductibles for private coverage. She also repositions some of her retirement assets into cash reserves to reduce exposure of her short-term income to the market she leverages her dollars prior to retirement, to secure long-term care coverage so that she is not a burden to her children in the event of her health failing. Because she has adequate cash reserves, her deductible is raised, which lowers her premium.

She will leave the school for the last time thinking only about the adventures she will have. She meets with me annually to review and make sure we're still on track.

The success of any financial plan is dependent upon the lifestyle we choose, relative to the lifestyle we can afford. Every financial goal is a factor of Money + Time + Rate of Return. If we break this formula down, the only two components we can control are the time and the money.

Time and money each have two components, which are "in" and "out." How much money can you afford to put in (towards your goal)? How much will you commit to? How much money do you need to be able to take out (at some point in the future)? How much time do you have before you need the money? How long can you commit to funding the goal? How long does it need to last when you start taking money out?

The most difficult realization for most of us, especially during the stock market boom of the late 90's, is that we cannot pin our hopes and dreams on unrealistic rates of return. The equation is simple; the problem is that most of us don't want to make the lifestyle changes necessary to balance the equation in our favor.

I challenge you to protect yourselves and your families before you spend another dime on stuff that doesn't matter! Paying yourself first is the ultimate money back guarantee.

Chapter 21
Personal Disaster

I was driving our family's conversion van on I-64, twenty-four miles outside of Mt. Vernon, Illinois. Behind me was our Audi on a tow-dolly. We were moving from West Virginia, where I had been a prison chaplain, to Bremerton, Washington, where I was going on active duty with the Navy. Our two youngest kids were sleeping on the fold down bed. Things seemed good.

I glanced out my extended rear-view mirror. *Smoke!* And the smoke was following me. I asked my wife to look out the right mirror.

"Where's that smoke coming from?" she asked.

I pulled to the side of the road, shut off the engine, got down on my hands and knees and looked under the van. *Fire!* Transmission fluid was squirting onto the hot exhaust manifold and flaming. The flaming fluid was running under the van. One tire was already on fire.

I got up and swung open the door. "Janis, get the kids and get out – the van is on fire!" I yelled.

Two truckers from Top Gun Trucking ran up and expended their fire extinguishers but it didn't help. I ran to the back of the van, opened the rear doors and was able to toss out a box and suitcase. Then the flaming fluid ran between my feet, and I had to give up.

One of the truckers handed me $200, put his hand on my shoulder and said, "Son, your van's a goner. I'm sorry for you and your family. We got to get back on the road." They carted their empty fire extinguishers to their rigs and drove off.

It took the volunteer fire department nearly half-an-hour to arrive— by that time both vehicles were totaled. My uniforms were burned. All of the Christmas decorations my wife had made by hand were destroyed. Each of our four children lost something personal and cherished.

Kind people drove my wife and three of our kids to a Holiday Inn. My oldest son and I rode with the tow truck to the wrecking yard, and then met up with the rest of the family.

"Uh-oh, my travelers' checks were burned up in the van."

Thankfully, the manager at the Holiday Inn understood.

A family from a Mt. Vernon church heard of our predicament, as did a dentist. Both contacted their pastors. They brought warm clothing and food to my family. The local family invited us to their house for Thanksgiving and their church took an offering for us. The dentist paid for a van to drive us to the St. Louis airport. Our unexpected four day stay in Mt Vernon, IL was made pleasant by these generous people.

UNDERSTANDING THE CRISIS

It's difficult to define or explain what a disaster is. For purposes of this book, I'll say that a disaster is an event that displaces a family unexpectedly. It also causes the family financial hardship. The disaster could be caused by fire, flood, or a natural weather phenomenon such as a tornado or hurricane. I have also seen families displaced by their homes being considered crime scenes. The disastrous event will probably have affected their home, business, or car. Periodically a school is involved in a disaster; however, schools have procedures in place for disaster recovery.

Often these disasters cause death, and then Post Traumatic Stress Syndrome in one or more people.

The primary things to consider when helping in a disaster situation is that the family needs shelter or transportation (or both), food, money, school supplies, phones, cooking utensils, hygiene products, and these are just immediate needs. In the near future they'll need more of these, and probably furniture, alternate season clothing, beds, appliances, prescription medications, and many other items. Most families have insurance, but quite a few are under-insured.

In home fires and other disasters families suffer the loss of treasured items. Generally people who haven't suffered a loss such as this will say the items are just "things." However, many of the "things" are family heirlooms like pictures of deceased family members, handmade items, mementos, things that can never be replaced. People will grieve these losses. The same can be said if the family loses a pet in the disaster—they will grieve.

APPLICABLE SCRIPTURE

Blessed are the merciful, for they will be shown mercy.

—Matthew 5:7

We have different gifts, according to the grace given us. If it is serving, let him serve; ... if it is encouraging, let him encourage; if it is contributing to the needs of others, let him give generously; ... if it is showing mercy, let him do it cheerfully.

—Romans 12:6A, 7A, 8

WHAT TO PRAY FOR

- Pray for anyone injured in the disaster.
- If the family was insured, pray their insurance comes through quickly.

- If no one was injured, praise and thank God.

- Pray for and thank God for the generosity of others.

HOW TO HELP

Pastors are called in to help in disasters. My experience is, like in my situation, it was people we had never met that came to our aid. Perhaps that's because of my military background.

Be aware of agencies in your area that respond to disasters. The Salvation Army and the American Red Cross are the two most well known and experienced. Both have relief funds for food and shelter. In areas where neither exists, your pastor will probably have knowledge of who to contact.

You should make a list of things the family needs. In a total disaster the needs are evident. You will immediately want to concentrate on clothing sizes and sexes of the family, food and shelter, and any necessary medications.

In the event of death, serious injury, or the death of a pet, counseling, especially PTSD, should be implemented. Counseling will reduce anxiety, help speed emotional normalcy, and if the event resulted from someone's neglect, may help heal relationships.

You, as a church leader, friend, or family member, should consider accompanying the family back to their damaged home, business, or car. The return will most likely be emotionally draining, and the comfort of your presence will be helpful. During this period the family will express many emotions. They may be in shock. Your primary role will be to listen and encourage. You may also be called upon to drive, cook, and collect clothing. All of these will be beneficial to the family.

One final consideration is the emotional exhaustion of the family. This may not happen to all families, but it usually does. Even though I was experienced at working disasters, I was emotionally exhausted from working my own. Having the church family and the dentist in Mt. Vernon, IL collect items for us, provide meals, and drive us to church and other necessary places took a burden off of me. I concentrated on moving my family the rest of the way to Washington. I had so many things to think about, and no funds for two days until the travelers checks were replaced, that I was overloaded. My point in saying this is to watch for emotional exhaustion in the family or friends you are working with.

Signs of emotional exhaustion are family infighting, poor decision making, lack of focusing, lack of motivation, feeling overstressed. Your help and comforting presence will help considerably.

Chapter 22
Friend/Relative
Incarcerated

The phone on my desk made the familiar double ring telling me the call originated from outside the prison.

"Chaplain's office, Chaplain Scott speaking. May I help you?"

"Good morning, Chaplain. I am Bishop Paul Jones from The Savior's Tabernacle in the Bronx. How are you today?"

"Good, Bishop, what can I do for you?" I asked wondering if I had heard from him or of him. "Chaplain, I heard from my son that he was being transferred to your prison. That was a while back, maybe three weeks ago, and we haven't heard from him since." My stomach tightened before he went on. "I was hoping you could help me."

"Bishop, I'm sorry. It's the policy of the Federal Bureau of Prisons (FBOP) not to let employees confirm or deny if an inmate is at a facility." I knew this hurt him, it would have hurt me. This policy is for the safety and security of facilities and inmates.

"Is there anyone I can call?" He sounded like a concerned parent, and I really did want to help. I told him I'd transfer him to the front desk where they would give him the information number for FBOP.

"Before you do that, may I ask you a question?"

"Sure you may. I hope it's a question I'm allowed to answer."

"Chaplain, we raised our son in a good Christian home. He learned all about the Bible and could recite verses, sing hymns and praise songs. He even played in our church band." I could hear anguish in his voice. "Now, Chaplain, he not only got himself in trouble, but he's gone and joined up with a religious group I've never heard of. What is going on with our son?"

"Well, Bishop, I don't know that I know your son." I paused to catch myself before he might say his son's name. "But I will tell you that it's common for inmates to change religions while incarcerated." That usually didn't help a parent in a circumstance such as this, but it let them know they weren't alone in the situation.

"Why do they do it?" he questioned.

"Various reasons—for some individuals it's to make a clean break from their past. Others do it to fit into a certain group, still others because they like the volunteers who come in from outside to lead the services of the group." I had about fifteen separate groups in the facility.

"Is there anything you can do to help change him back?" He was pleading with me, looking for a sense of security for his son.

"Bishop, chaplains in the Bureau aren't allowed to try and change another person's religion in the performance of their duties. I'm sorry."

The bishop exhaled loudly. "Am I allowed to try when I come for a visit?"

"Certainly, Bishop, and I hope to meet you if he's here."

UNDERSTANDING THE CRISIS

Families of inmates in jails or prisons face their own special anguish. They feel they have failed as parents. Now the time they spend with their loved one is limited, and often is separated by Plexiglas, and muffled by an intercom or by conversation through a few holes drilled through the Plexiglas. As visitors they are often searched or pass through a security screening. Correctional officers and TV cameras monitor the visit.

When visiting a prison facility to visit the relative, family members note that correctional officers (guards) tend to seem untrusting. If face-to-face contact is allowed, correctional officers may warn family members to maintain a distance and not to touch, except for a brief hug and/or kiss at the end of the visit. This is to prevent contraband (drugs and weapons) from entering the prison. One of the most common ways contraband enters is through family or friend's visits. Mail is also opened and screened. All of this is done for the safety of the staff and inmates.

Family members are often unprepared for their relative/inmate's attitude changes. They initially go through anger, depression, serious fear, and several other emotions, attitudes, and feelings. If the family cooperated with authorities the inmate may take years to get over feelings of betrayal. Since families feel that their inmate/relative betrayed family values by committing crimes, relations are generally tense.

Inmates tend to feel powerless, fearful, and a lack of control. In many cases doomed where lengthy sentences are involved. Prison authorities like the inmates to feel powerless and a lack of control. The wardens and their staffs need total control to maintain the safety and security of the facility. Where inmates gain power and some control, staff and inmates are injured and often die.

Inmates often have their housing changed, job assignments changed, or may be transferred to other facilities with little or no notice if the warden's staff feels it is necessary for the security of the institution [for instance, to break up a group or gang, or to increase an inmates security level].

There are many high quality prison ministries. Some, such as Prison Fellowship, are national. Many churches and other organizations operate local prison and jail ministries. There are also many biblical correspondence courses at little or no cost to inmates. Many of the inmates I knew who were taking courses benefited from them.

Prison may provide excellent opportunities for increased growth in faith, especially when there is help from the outside, and a supportive family.

APPLICABLE SCRIPTURE

I was in prison and you came to visit me.

—Matthew 25:36c

Remember those in prison as if you were their fellow prisoners.

—Hebrews 13:3a

WHAT TO PRAY FOR

- Pray for the safety and security of those in prison.
- Pray for increased faith in God for the inmate(s).
- Pray for the repentance and salvation of your relative.
- Pray for justice in the event your relative was wrongly convicted.
- Pray that your family will overcome obstacles and be reunited.
- As strange as it may sound, pray for the warden and his/her staff.

HOW TO HELP

Your greatest responsibility in helping a church member, family member, or friend, whose relative is in prison or jail, is to give encouragement. This encouragement will fall into two areas:

First, if it is their child who is incarcerated, they will need support in knowing they haven't failed as parents, and that there is hope for their child.

Second, your position is to encourage them to operate within the legal limits of the institution where their relative is incarcerated.

Some institutions allow books, tapes, videos, CDs, and other religious materials to be sent into the institution, within limits and guidelines, while others don't allow items sent in at all. Learn what is and is not allowed and encourage your family member to send support. For instance, where I worked hardback books were not permitted whereas paperback and leather Bibles were allowed.

Encourage them to send religious materials, if possible, and only so long as their relative reads them or listens to them. As inmates tend to have a lot of spare time, I also encourage sending periodicals.

Help your friend or family to accept that they don't know, and most likely won't know and understand, the culture inside the prison. Inmates as a whole have a vastly different value system, moral code, view of the justice system, and "pecking order" than you will ever see anywhere else. When they voice their opinion on it, they shouldn't be shocked or surprised if their opinion is forcefully rejected. Living by the inmate value system and moral code, along with the pecking order, may mean survival to the inmate.

Holidays are particularly emotionally difficult for inmates and their families. They tend to feel extremely depressed at Christmas, birthdays, and other major event dates. Relatives should program visits during these periods.

Encourage your relatives to try their best to maintain contact with their relative—they will always be family.

There is a difference between how men and women react to prison. The most difficult part of being locked up for men is the loss of freedom. For women, it is the separation from family, especially from their children.

There is a controversy over whether or not taking children to see their parent in prison is a good idea. Each child, each family, and each inmate is different. I recommended it in some cases, and recommended against it in others. Mostly, it depends on the attitude of the inmate. If he/she is a loving parent and does their best to maintain contact with the child, then I recommend visits if the child handles the visits well.

If the parent acts aloof or uncaring, I recommend against the visits unless the child is older and can emotionally handle the visits; otherwise the child should stay away.

A final consideration is how well the child can deal with the prison setting. The women's prison where I was a chaplain had no towers, no armed guards, and looked like a college campus. It even had a playground for the kids. However, children may be traumatized by a facility with armed guards, towers, razor wire, and barriers. This is also a good consideration when taking elderly people to visit.

If you or your relative is interested in providing prison or jail ministry I encourage you to become involved in a ministry that provides excellent training such as Prison Fellowship. I will caution you, however, that most prisons and jails will not allow you to minister inside a facility where you have a relative. Again, it is a security issue.

Warning: If you do become involved in a prison ministry, beware of becoming personally involved with inmates other than your relatives. Established prison ministries such as Prison Fellowship, forbid it. Inmates have scammed many people, and most victims I know were fairly new to volunteering at the prison. Not all inmates are scammers, but until you develop enough savvy and experience to tell, which will take you about a decade, err on the side of caution. Even professional prison workers sometimes get scammed.

I recommend you avoid being scammed by not sending money for the inmate. Instead, buy and send items. I know of cases where inmates requested money to purchase a Bible, and instead purchased cigarettes or subscribed to porn magazines. Money was also used to pay for tattoos, gambling debts, etc. Contact the chaplain and find out how to have a Bible sent in to the inmate if they want one.

Often volunteers and visitors become emotionally involved with inmates—only to find out the inmate is married, or carrying on with several other supporter/lovers. Shy away from personal involvement.

Having a relative in prison can put a strain on a family, especially if a child (even adult child) is involved. Try to avoid the "blame game" against family members. Counseling for the parents is beneficial and recommended.

Chapter 23
Lawsuit - Being Sued

While walking on our main street in the small town in Alaska where I was a pastor, I encountered a good friend. "Lonnie, you're not going to believe what happened to me," he exclaimed.

"It doesn't sound good so far, Don. You don't look or sound good at all."

"During our first opener of the season [legal commercial fishing period], I went to help another fisherman. The weather was getting rough and I accidentally drifted over another fella's net, keeping the one guy off the rocks." He pulled out an old handkerchief, pretending to wipe his nose he wiped a tear from his eye. "Anyway, he's suing me for the cost of an entire net, and what he figures he lost in fish."

"Oh, Don, I'm sorry to hear that." Don was a wonderful man, always helping others. I couldn't imagine anyone suing or otherwise hurting him.

"That's not the worst part of it, Lonnie."

"What else is there?"

"The man who is suing is a Christian. I asked if we could do a Christian mediation and he said he wouldn't."

I was stunned.

UNDERSTANDING THE CRISIS

A civil lawsuit is a court action taken by one party against another party to correct a real or perceived wrong. A party may be a person, group of people, government, organization, company, just about anyone.

The parties in a civil suit are the plaintiff or the person bringing about the lawsuit perceiving himself/herself to have been wronged, and the defendant, who is the person being accused of committing the wrong.

A wrong might be money owed for goods or services not provided, for an injury, for loss of property due to damage or theft, slander, violating a contract, or many other situations. In the story we see where Don damaged another man's property, and caused the other man loss of income.

Procedures for court actions vary from state to state in cases where small amounts of money are concerned. Small claims courts have set limits, for example $1,000.00 may be the limit in a state. If the suit is for $1,000.00 or less, the case will be heard before a judge. Attorneys are not used; each party in the suit represents themselves before the judge. Currently there are several television shows depicting small claim court cases.

For larger claims the parties are more likely to have attorneys and have their cases heard before a jury. Judgments are not, as in a criminal trial, a guilty or not-guilty verdict. Rather, in a civil case the judge brings a judgment for either the plaintiff or defendant. Another difference from a criminal trial is that the jury doesn't have to be unanimous in their vote. Juries vary by state and may consist of fewer than twelve people depending on the state.

There are biblical directions for Christians involved in lawsuits. Those directions primarily involve Christians suing one another in public court. While it is lawful for Christians to sue, including bringing suits against other Christians, the Bible asks us to do otherwise. Christians are actually to be held to a higher standard.

Consider these three points when examining the issue of using the secular legal system to resolve disputes:

1. The principle of forgiveness is to be practiced as Jesus taught it should be (Matthew 6:14–15; also consider the parable in Matthew 18:21–35).

2. The secular system is being used to judge the righteous, when in

actuality our standards are to be higher and more righteous.

3. We are poor example to the world. Jesus said that we are to be a city set upon a hill to light up the world (Matthew 5:14–16). If we act unforgiving, greedy, angry, or heartless, what does that teach the world about Christians?

Our first consideration should be to bring glory to God. This, in fact could cause some people not to sue, and lose money—I acknowledge that. There have been four times I could have sued people due to either injuries suffered, or where someone cheated or otherwise wronged me. I went to the people, explained my position, and forgave them. By doing so Christ was glorified and the Church was built up rather than brought down. The money I could have gained would never have achieved the same result.

A man in a church I pastored was seeking a settlement in a lawsuit. He made the remark, "Just think of the tithe off that amount." It was a substantial sum of money, but I told him I didn't want the money.

In each case mentioned here, God blessed either my family, or in the last case, the church by taking the "higher road" and following the principles taught in the Bible.

If in fact our standards are higher, our judgments are righteous, and our Christian values and principles are taken to heart, then what do we do if we are wronged?

The answer I propose is Christian mediation. Using Christian mediation accomplishes several things for you, your family member, or friend, which a secular court would not be able to do.

First, it puts the parties into contact with strong, wise Christians, quite possibly elders in local churches if the dispute is settled locally. The biblical wisdom gleaned from them is valuable beyond the measure of money. I have heard of Christians growing as a result of this type of mediation.

Second, it keeps the dispute out of courts where embarrassment is painful to Christians and the Church as a whole. Further, the dispute will probably be settled far more quickly—often in a matter of days or weeks, rather than months or years as in the case of the court system.

Third, you, your family member, or friend will save thousands of dollars in court costs and attorney fees. There may be some expenses if a person or people are summoned from one of the Christian mediation organizations, but the expenses will be far less than taking the dispute to secular court. In the area where I live, attorney fees generally start at $5,000 and go up from there. When a person loses a court case they often have to pay both sides' fees. When a person wins a court case the attorneys on the winning side generally receive thirty to forty percent of the money awarded.

One final thought I have on this matter is that we, as Americans, have rights and we are used to using these rights (and there may be brothers and sisters from other countries who have many of the same rights). These rights have sometimes conflicted with Christian values. For instance, we have, according to the Fifth Amendment of the Constitution, the right to refuse to speak when we are accused of something. But if we know we are guilty of doing something wrong, or if we know what we are doing is offensive to someone, should invoking a Constitutional right, or claiming we have a right to do something be invoked? What does that do for the cause of Christ? I have another story to tell, which may shed light on this.

Marvin was a man in my church who had led a hard life. Alcohol, drugs, fights—you name it—Marvin was involved. Then late one night, Marvin dedicated his heart to the Lord. A few weeks later Marvin came to me and told me he was wanted for crimes in another state, and that he was flying there the next day. We prayed for him that night and asked God to protect him. Marvin strolled into court, unexpectedly, definitely not on the docket, and asked to turn himself in. The judge asked what he was doing there. Marvin explained everything, including the part that he was guilty. He also gave his Christian testimony. The judge dismissed the charges against him.

This is not to say this will happen to everyone, I know that is not true from my experience as a prison chaplain, but God is going rain down blessings on those who live their faith.

APPLICABLE SCRIPTURE

If your brother sins against you, go and show him his fault, just between the two of you. If he listens to you, you have won your brother over. But if he will not listen, take one or two others along, so that "every matter may be established by the testimony of two or three witnesses." If he refuses to listen to them, tell it to the church; and if he refuses to listen even to the church, treat him as you would a pagan or a tax collector. I tell you the truth, whatever you bind on earth will be bound in heaven, and whatever you loose on earth will be loosed in heaven.

—Matthew 18:15–18

If any among you has a dispute with another, dare he take it before the ungodly for judgment instead of before the saints? Do you not know that the saints will judge the world? And if you are to judge the world, are you not competent to judge trivial cases? Do you not know that we will judge the angels? How much more are the things of this life! Therefore, if you have disputes about such matters, appoint as judges even men of little account in the church! I say this to shame you. Is it possible that there is nobody among you wise enough to judge a dispute between believers? But instead, one brother goes to law against another brother—and this in front of unbelievers! The very fact that you have lawsuits among you means you have been completely defeated already. Why not rather be wronged? Why not rather be cheated? Instead, you yourselves cheat and do wrong, and you do this to your brothers.

—1 Corinthians 6:1–8

I would also suggest reading Exodus 18, where Jethro advises Moses to appoint "capable" men to act as judges among the people, and Matthew 18:21–35, the parable of the unmerciful servant.

WHAT TO PRAY FOR

- Pray for the parties to practice forgiveness.
- Pray for the leadership of the church leaders.
- Pray for wisdom for the mediators.

HOW TO HELP

For the non-Christian friend or family member

Helping a friend or family member in a legal matter first entails advising them that you will help them only so far as they are honest. Any time they become deceptive, I highly recommend you back away.

I strongly recommend that you not give legal advice. This is especially true if someone has become involved in a criminal case. Anytime I have been to visit someone in the brig or jail, or while serving as prison chaplain, and someone asked a question about legal procedure, I told them to follow their attorney's advice. At some point you may have been involved in a similar type case, whether civil or criminal, however, since laws or procedures may have changed, or there may be enough of a difference in the cases that you could unknowingly hurt the person.

For the Christian friend or family member:

When it comes to helping a Christian friend or family member, encourage them to closely study the Scripture passages given previously in this chapter. Ask them to search their heart and look deep for unforgiveness, vengeance, hate and anything else unchristian, and remove it from their life. Ask them to read 1 Corinthians 13 and Galatians 5:22–26 with you. If that fails, I recommend the following options.

If your church member, family member or friend is suing a non-Christian, encourage them to seek a Christian attorney who upholds Biblical values.

If your family member, parishioner, or friend is intent on suing a Christian, encourage them to seek mediation through church pastors or elders. If the parties all go to the same church, the situation could be rectified in a quick, easy, quiet, inexpensive, and most importantly, scriptural way.

If the parties do not go to the same church, there are three ways the situation could be resolved:

1. Having the pastors or elders from the churches act as mediators

2. Asking the pastor or elders from a third church to act as mediators

3. Seeking resolution from a Christian mediation service

Options one and two are self-explanatory. The process can be kept simple, and the elders selected need to be totally impartial, spiritual, and whose primary goal is to glorify God using biblical values and judgments. I would keep the number of elders from perhaps three to seven. After hearing the parties, and if necessary, witnesses, I would dismiss everyone from the room. Have the elders vote secretly, and have the vote told to the parties. I would recommend against revealing the pattern of the vote, knowing that would serve no useful purpose.

Prior to the start of the meeting, the elder selected to chair the mediation should explain the process, including the voting procedure, to the parties. Have the parties agree that one the judgment is revealed the dispute will go no further.

The Christian mediation services I made contact with are distinct in their operations from each other.

ICORVI (from 1Cor6) helps in the mediation process by bringing the parties and church members/mediators together, teaching and training them to settle the dispute (ICORVI 1-800-747-6655 or www. icorvi.org). Once a dispute is known, they come in and get the mediation moving, but they do not participate in the process.

Peacemaker Ministries trains local churches how to have mediation available and ready (Peacemaker Ministries 1-406-256-1583 or www. peacemaker.net). They are trainers, and have several courses to train members of churches in understanding and settling disputes.

FOLLOW UP

When Don's pastor returned from a church conference, Don went to him and explained the circumstance. Don's pastor then went to the pastor of the man suing and explained it to him. The two pastors and

Don then met with the man and discussed the circumstances which occurred on the water, as well as the ramifications of the lawsuit. The man whose boat needed to be rescued was then brought in to discuss splitting the cost of the damages. When he heard about the situation, he offered to pay for the net and for a portion of the fish that were lost. Don was absolved of paying anything.

Chapter 24
Church Split/Conflict

While I was in seminary the church my family and I attended went through a split. This was a painful time for all concerned. It caused conflict in families, friendships, and professional relationships. In one family I befriended, the mother continued to attend the church, the adult son moved to another church, and the adult daughter quit attending church altogether.

The pain many in the congregation experienced was also felt by some in the leadership, but those in pain felt ignored by the church leadership. The situation was not managed well because the leadership did not take a strong lead toward a healthy resolution.

I won't go into the details of the cause of the conflict of that particular church, as the church still exists. However, the leadership has changed in the years since I attended, and I continue to pray for the work they are doing in the name of Christ.

UNDERSTANDING THE CRISIS

Most church conflicts and splits aren't pretty. Once in a while conflict brings about a positive change in a church, and occasionally a split results in two successful churches rather than just one. This is not the type of conflict I am discussing here.

Conflicts occur for many reasons. Generally, it boils down to the expectations of the members not being met. Oddly, expectations at work, home, or elsewhere may contribute to this, but an easy place to lay blame for their discontent is with the church, the pastor, staff members, or programs.

Conflicts and splits in the church tend to have negative impacts for a long while, and tend to be quite ugly. There are three primary reasons why I say they are ugly: (1) people get hurt, (2) they aren't always for "gospel" reasons, and (3) they generally aren't managed well.

Many people put their faith and hope in their local church or pastor rather than in the Gospel. They view their church or pastor as the sole dispenser of the Gospel. So when conflict arises in church, and the actions or beliefs of their pastor are called into question, their world comes crashing down. They may literally feel a part of them has died. This happens because people are not discipled properly to follow the lead of Christ and the written Word of God over a pastor or a church.

Another reason for pain in a church split is that people donate many years of their lives, tithes and offerings, to the work of the church. When a split occurs, they feel as though they have wasted their resources, much the same way a worker feels when laid off after investing years to a company or business.

Churches have had conflicts and splits for some of the worst reasons you can imagine: the color of the new carpet, whether to pave the parking lot, changing the service time to one hour later, and other such reasons. I recall hearing about a large, successful church going through a nasty split due to disagreement over using an overhead projector to display songs rather than purchase new hymnals. The person who told this to me was the former pastor who resigned in disgust and became a Navy chaplain, and a very successful one I might add.

There are specific times when churches might have conflict. Some of those times are: during a staffing change, during membership or funds drives, during a change in programs, during an influx of new members or attendees—especially if the new people are of a different generation than the majority of the established members.

When looking specifically at splits, there are some good reasons for church splits to occur. One is when a certain individual or group of people has a disagreement over theological views held by the church, or denomination. Another reason is if an individual or group is in disagreement with the direction the church leadership is going. There are good and proper ways for departure from the church. We will discuss these in the HOW TO HELP section.

255

Another good reason for a split is the formation of another church due to the current church being overcrowded. I witnessed this when I was attending Bible College. The church we attended had two Sunday morning services in which both were crowded. The leadership asked the assistant pastor to take a portion of the congregation and form a new church in an area where a "like church" didn't exist. They sent a portion of the leadership, teachers, and worship team with him, and supported the work financially. Several people I knew were against this (though a very small percentage) due to separating the leadership, but their views were heard, and their opposing views were addressed in a Christian manner.

APPLICABLE SCRIPTURE

You are still worldly. For since there is jealousy and quarreling among you, are you not worldly? Are you not acting like mere men? For when one says, "I follow Paul," and another, "I follow Apollos," are you not mere men?

What, after all, is Apollos? And what is Paul? Only servants, through whom you came to believe—as the Lord has assigned to each his task. I planted the seed, Apollos watered it, but God made it grow.

—1 Corinthians 3:3–6

The acts of the sinful nature are obvious: ... discord ... jealousy ... dissentions ... factions and envy.

—Galatians 5:19–20

It was he who gave some to be apostles, some to be prophets, some to be evangelists, and some to be pastors and teachers, to prepare God's people for works of service, so that the body of Christ may be built up until we all reach unity in the faith and in the knowledge of the Son of God and become mature, attaining to the whole measure of the fullness of Christ.

Then we will no longer be infants, tossed back and forth by the waves, and blown here and there by every wind of teaching and by the cunning and craftiness of men in their deceitful scheming. Instead, speaking the truth in love, we will in all things grow up into him who is the Head, that is, Christ. From him the whole body, joined and held together by every supporting ligament, grows and builds itself up in love, as each part does its work.

—Ephesians 4:11–16

To the elders among you, I appeal as a fellow elder, a witness of Christ's sufferings and one who also will share in the glory to be revealed: Be shepherds of God's flock that is under your care, serving as overseers—not because you must, but because you are willing, as God wants you to be; not greedy for money, but eager to serve; not lording it over those entrusted to you, but being examples to the flock. Young men, in the same way be submissive to those who are older. All of you, clothe yourselves with humility toward one another.

—1 Peter 5:1–3, 5a

WHAT TO PRAY FOR

- Pray for the pastors and elders.
- Pray for those who dissent with the leadership.
- Pray for the specific cause of dissent.
- Pray for those who are considering leaving the church due to the turmoil.
- If a split occurs, pray for unity for those who remain.
- Pray that conflict will be dealt with in a Godly manner.

PROCEDURES

I realize there is more than one style of church policy, however I am writing this primarily to the elder style of leadership. It will fit all types found in the Protestant church.

We all have to realize that church conflicts and splits are inevitable. They happen for various reasons: doctrinal issues, changes in leadership, disagreements with the direction the church is going, etc. We should realize that conflict may have a positive impact on the church if it is dealt with in a positive and healthy manner. Churches are often motivated to make positive changes when someone attempts to bring about change. Seeking a positive resolution should be at the forefront of everyone's mind involved in the conflict. Attempting to sidestep the issues, ignore the conflict, or silence dissatisfied parties will only make matters worse. Conflict not dealt with, or an impending split ignored or mismanaged, results in a dysfunctional church.

From the leadership position, pastors and elders must realize they aren't going to please everyone. Not everyone is going to be happy with the pastor's style of preaching, methods of leadership and management, and not everyone is going to be energized by his vision. In addition, not everyone is going to be pleased with the manner in which the elders vote, the results of their voting, or the way they supervise.

Those in positions of visibility such as the Sunday school superintendents, worship team leaders, choir members, and Sunday school teachers, may find themselves targets of conflict or be asked to take sides.

The following points should be used when conflict arises to attempt to resolve it:

1. The parties in conflict should not look at each other as enemies or adversaries, but as brothers and sisters in Christ.

2. The parties in conflict should make every attempt to understand the other side's point of view—understanding does not necessarily mean agreement, but it helps when seeking resolution.

3. The parties in conflict should seek resolution between themselves. Christians have been empowered by Jesus to resolve conflicts between themselves (Matthew 18:15).

4. If the parties are unable to settle the conflict, I recommend the elders be called in to attempt to settle the issue. Remember this is not a courtroom, and the objective is not to decide one party is wrong while the other is right. Rather, both sides should present their issue and answer the elders' questions, then step out while the elders discuss the issues and vote. If possible, a mutually agreeable third position should be sought.

5. The party for whom the vote was against should have the reason(s) for the vote carefully explained to them.

6. The party for whom the vote was against then needs to decide between one of two choices: (a) remain in the church quietly, or (b) leave the church quietly. No one has the right to be a disruptive member of the church. If the party is dissatisfied with the outcome of the elders vote, then they should seek a church to their liking, or barring that, start their own church.

7. If the party decides to leave, or if the party was more than one person and part of them decides to leave, the church should refrain from speaking negatively about them. I have witnessed this happen, and it appears, even to outsiders, unchristian. Also if the party decides to return, they won't feel welcome if they heard the church was speaking negatively about them.

Splits are going to be painful to a church. Splits often result in a change of pastor or other staff member, lower offerings, loss of Sunday school teachers, loss of key members, work not getting done, and other affects. However, the damage done by a split can be minimized if the church manages it well. Here are some final suggestions:

1. Do not keep the congregation in the dark. Treat the congregation as adults by telling them what is occurring. Many probably

already sense something is wrong, and informing them cuts down on rumors, speculations, and departures.

2. Treat those who are departing as brothers and sisters in Christ, and never as an enemy. An amiable split brings glory to Christ—a bitter split causes the true enemy a victory.

3. If a new church is formed as a result of the split, and the established church has abundant resources, I recommend sharing the resources if the new church is doctrinally sound. Again, this brings glory to Christ.

During all phases of conflict or split, all individuals involved should bear in mind that Christ established the Church—He is the Head of all—every action taken should be taken with the intent to bring Him glory.